Alba gu bràth
Scotland forever

Cher Bonfis

Independence Missives

Cher Bonfis: - Was born in Speakers House when William Morrision was Speaker of The House of Commons. Cher's mother was a cleaning woman in the Houses of Parliament who cleaned up for four House of Commons Speakers. After which she and her family returned to Paisley where she ran her own cleaning business called 'Speakers Cleaners'…. Sorry that was a lie… Is it worth beginning again? Probably not, for the words written here, or in some newspaper, would not really allow you to access the mind of this author. If you want to know about this person best you read the things this person writes. Trivia over details of this life are irrelevant. What you should know is that there is much gratitude for your interest and there is hope that you have found something rewarding. If you believe in love and kindness. If you believe everyone deserves a chance to live a happy life then you and Cher Bonfis have a lot in common. Word by word we will strive to make things better. So thank you for stopping by, and may all good things be yours.

Independence Missives

Cher Bonfis

Lulach Publishing

Cher Bonfis

Published by Lulach Publishing 2023

https://www.lulachpublishing.com

Cher Bonfis
Independence Missives

British Library cataloguing in Publication Data. A Catalogue record for this book is available from the British Library.

ISBN 978-1-7396723-7-9

BIC categories:- JP, JF, KC,

Typeset in Elatan and Gaelic

PB

The missives presented in this book
were written as social media posts
and letters to 'The National Newspaper',
of Scotland during 2021 and 2022.
They document the history of these years,
and offer some ideas to forward our quest.
for Scottish Independence
Alba gu bràth - Scotland forever

Cher Bonfis

I believe that money is simply the tool to keep
us masses in our place. The top 5% have
lashings of the stuff they can come, go and do
as they will. The rest of us have to come, go
and do the bidding of the top 5% otherwise we
have no roof, food or clothes.

From Margaret Thatcher's book
'The Downing Street Years'

"The Tory Party is not, of course, an English party, but a Unionist one. If it sometimes seems English to some Scots, that is because the Union is inevitably dominated by England by reason of its greater population. The Scots, being an historic nation with a proud past, will inevitably resent some expressions of this fact from time to time.

"As a nation, they have an undoubted right to national self-determination; thus far they have exercised that right by joining and remaining in the Union. Should they determine on independence, no English party or politician would stand in their way, however much we might regret their departure."

François-Marie Arouet
Voltaire

We look to Scotland for all our ideas on
civilisation

Samuel Johnson

Oats: A grain, which in
England is generally given to horses,
but in Scotland supports the people

JM Barrie

There are few more impressive sights in the world than a Scotsman on the make

Winston Churchill

Of all small nations of this earth, perhaps only the ancient Greeks surpass the Scots in their contribution to mankind

George Bernard Shaw

God help England if she had no
Scots to think for her

Nicola Sturgeon

Scotland almost invented the modern world.
I mean, all of these televisions, telephones,
penicillin, we all — all of these things were
invented in Scotland.

Cher Bonfis

Elections
Social Media Post 06 May 2021

Elections for Holyrood next week are serious. It is time for us to stand and become all that we can be once more an independent European nation.

Unionists will say 'GERS deficit' but will fail to mention that the Westminster Government wish to be the 'Continuing State' after Scottish Independence. In simple terms that means they will keep all the assets of the current set up, like overseas territory embassies, various rights to this and that AND THEY ALSO TAKE ALL THE DEBT….. If Scotland decides to become Independent, Independent Scotland would start with a clean slate. WHY? The rest of the UK want to keep the seat at the United Nations Security Council.

There will be a border they will cry…..So what? There are borders all over the world. New ones crop up all the time. There is a new one between Northern Ireland and the rUK, it just popped up out of the Irish sea when no one was looking. Surely it has caused grief and it will cause more but it has had a positive economic benefit for the Northern Ireland economy and still the Unionists rant against it. The ingenuity of humans will work out ways to profit from any new border in the long term, in the short term the spanking, brand new border created by Brexit, between Scotland and Europe, has crashed Scottish Fish Exporters businesses, we will see if they can find a way to survive.

There will be loud shouts that we Scots sell more in the UK Market than in Europe. They fail to mention that some of those sales will have been reliant upon onward trade to European destinations. They will fail to mention that Scots sell more to the rest of the world Than to the rest of the UK.

Politicians will suggest that Scotland needs the 'board shoulders' of the UK without mentioning that if Scotland had it's own Central Bank and full control of Taxation, Foreign Policy and Defence, Scottish shoulders would be just a board or broader.

Oh no one ever suggested we stop the 'Common Travel Area' which provides open borders between England, Scotland, Wales, Northern Ireland, The Isle of Man, The Channel Island's and Ireland. So free movement in these places will not change.   Of course before we were dragged from the European Union we had another twenty seven countries we could have travelled freely to live and work.

SNP-SNP Both Vote's

Alex Salmond

Our internationalism is the driver of our nationalism

20

Vote
Social Media Post 06 May 2021

It is election time in my country, democracy has it's chance once again today to progress. Only a few will hear the call of the ballot box. Many will think what is the point? Many will think I cannot make any difference. To them I would say how would you like me to write my next novel missing the page where finally all is revealed? Your vote is as important as that page in the book.

I just had a discussion about <u>one</u> word in my next book. The editor was all for changing <u>one</u> word 'their to his'! However, that one word change would have rendered the title of the book null and void and half of the possible culprits would have been eliminated before the reader had read the first paragraph!

We live in a world where there are many people who want to be top of the pile and those sorts of folk are just looking for a pile of other folk to climb on top of. As they ascend do they understand that without those they are climbing over there would be no top?

Democracy is challenged all the while, it may be that other systems yet to be invented will be better that it. At the moment the alternatives are displayed as dictatorship.

The lack of a substantial opposition is such a problem, a legitimate government needs a strong opposition to make it truly credible. If no real opposition exists and the race through the election to power did not even have to be run, how can the victor legitimately claim the victory?

I am not a fan of football but I guess there are teams from around the world who are so well known I could use them in this analogy. Suppose 'Manchester United' or 'Real Madrid' took their best squad of players to the park next Sunday and they played a match against some school kids, what would be the glory of a win for the big shot professionals?

So until we have a better, support Democracy at every turn and because the alternatives are even less pleasant, your vote is a page in the book and the story will hardly be recognisable without your page.

Winnie Ewing

The Scottish Parliament,
Adjorned on the 25th of March 1707
Is hereby reconvened

Independence
Social Media Post 18 September 2021

It is a day when we in Scotland who wish that we were an Independent country morn a little. For it was seven years ago today that we failed to gain enough votes to secure Independence at the last referendum. Today many in what we call the 'YES movement', that is YES we want Independence, have begun a fresh campaign to try and secure our Independence. The last referendum secured nothing much for Scotland. However it did secure "English Votes For English Laws", meaning that one outcome of the referendum was that whenever the Westminster parliament discuss laws which only effect the English; Scottish, Welsh and Northern Irish Ministers of Parliament have no say in what goes on. Just after the referendum votes were announced English political leaders made a 'VOW'. Our Scottish Parliament should have been enshrined in law. The Swell Convention should have been turned into law. Scotland's membership of the European Union should have been protected by making Scotland's membership the responsibility of the Scottish Parliament, Holyrood.

It has been half a century since Scotland had a UK Government which it voted for. There are supporters of the current Tory Government in Westminster here in Scotland but I, and many others, deplore the catalogue of reprehensible policies and laws, a list could go on for many pages, foisted upon Scotland by a government the majority of Scots did not vote for. Coupled with that Brexit has caused huge problems for Scottish Exporters, many EU citizens have returned to their own countries, having felt dislodged, means we now have not enough workers to do all that must be done. Supplies to our shops are sometimes short. The Conservative government's policy of 'Hostile Environment', to discourage refugees and economic migrants are felt by many Scots to be barbaric. There are also many reports of violence by police towards black people. The UK Government have not worked out how to implement the Northern Ireland Protocol, nor how to arrange for the checking of EU imports to the UK post Brexit. It could be thought that the UK Government is only interested in making money for rich people whilst many normal people live in squalor. There are terrible television news reports of some housing associations which fail to invest in repair and maintenance so that people have decent accommodation. Tenants pay have to pay high rents to live in slum conditions.

Scotland needs to have it's own Central Bank. It needs to control immigration, taxation, defence, pensions. We need to be back in the EU and be an outward looking, inclusive, and welcoming society, where the people and their well being are at the heart of what our government does.

Feeding the poor as Billionaires go into orbit
Social Media Post 2021

You heard that joke about Jeff, Richard, Elon, and Jared? No I did not think it that funny either. Pioneers? Well maybe. After all, man/woman has got to do what a man/woman has got to do! Break down the barriers, reach for the stars. Human kind can do it, but must they do it?

In Burundi there are around twelve million people. Most dwell in the countryside, they scratch a living by farming. They export coffee, tea and are subsidised by international donors. Half the children are malnourished. Worse, putting poverty aside, the 'World Happiness Report 2018', shows many people in Burundi feel dissatisfied with their lives, the country was rated the least happy in the world. They have had a good share of civil-wars and genocides. The soldiers have smart uniforms and guns, and their president has a big car. Many Burundian's do survive each year.

The question is how do we, the human race, support billionaire space flight and poverty that allows children to starve to death? The agricultural revelation of 12000 years ago, converted Sapiens from 'hunter-gatherers' into 'farmers'. He describes how this promised better lives for all but in reality the increased wealth of food gave rise to 'Elites' who creamed off the excess 'profits', whilst the 'ordinary' folk made more children and then had to work even harder to feed more mouths. So history continues. Populations rise and rise. Yin and yang. Rich and poor. Is it that the only way to make a billionaire is to make a lot more poor people? Or to make a lot more people poor?

Karl Marx provided a vision of class free societies, everyone equal. In practice the idyll fell somewhat short. The Indian Government sends rockets into space and holds an arsenal of nuclear weapons. It has almost one and a half billion people and sixty percent of them survive on less than four dollars a day. King Ludwig the Second of Bavaria had beautiful castles built, you may have heard of Neuschwanstein, construction started in 1869. The construction led him into debts of more than 14 million marks, about 90 million Euros today, but each year now 1 million 3 hundred thousand people visit it and they pay 15 Euros each to tour the splendid rooms of the palace.

The real question of our time is: How to we feed and house everyone and let billionaires fly into space. Whilst stopping the world from burning up in the climate crisis?

Your answers on a postcard please. I have none.

Cher Bonfis

Rishi Sunak's Budget does not have to balance unlike Scotland's

Also published in The National 30 October 2021 1

The English have a thing about being 'the best in the world', the first in the world, the biggest, the brightest. Of course they are not the only ones.

A claim is often made that Westminster is 'The Mother of Parliaments'. I suppose as the British Empire grow parliaments were forced into occupied territories, you can debate that if you want to. In the Westminster parliament the 'Chancellor of the Exchequer' turns up once a year with some 'hokus-pokus' and a crystal ball. He does a stand-up routine, fantasying about times, a few years from the day of his 'show'. He tries to convince people that what he suggests should be given credibility.

The first budget happened in 1284. In those far off times a chequered cloth was used to help them do the counting, hence the name. In that first budget they realised that the king, Edward I, Longshanks Hammer of the Scots, spent more money than he had income. By way of solution to this problem it was decided to tax people. Edward's minions were not were not the first to do that.

There was a budget today and it would have done some of the greatest comedians proud, if only they could have delivered such an hilarious show, 'Live at the Apollo', which is an English television show, on that he would have gone down a storm. The audience would have been rolling in the isles.

The chancellor claimed that the great pandemic 'give-a-way' of furlough, grants and loans has made not one jot of difference to the economy. More than that he claimed that Brexit has done nothing to dent the plucky 'Old English Bull Dog', still wagging his tail like a conductor at the 'Last Night of the Proms', land of hope and stories. In fact we were informed we are in the sunny climes of a period when spending on so many wonderful projects can go a head with abandon. There are some beauties to undermine Holyrood, but not the same amount of cash as would have been forthcoming from the European Union.

"It is ok everyone can feel fine and dandy. Remember you Scots, that this budget will level up the Union and never forget you could never do this alone. What would you Scottish people know about a Central Bank? It's called the 'Bank of England' you know! I never heard of Patterson, who was he?" The chancers teeth glistened for the television cameras.

It had been predicted that we would be borrowing so much more money then we actually have to! The current United Kingdom debt exceeds a mere 2 trillion pounds but the

Chancellor will borrow some more but not quite as much as expected. Thus the part time millionaire and aspiring film star, (surely that is true) said that "borrowing is under control". (Pause for audience laughter) However, just to make sure that all is 'Morally Correct', those who are unemployed will be a lot worse off tomorrow than they are today. After all there are plenty of jobs going, the country needs truck drivers and there is a dearth of night club bouncers. So get on your bike and find some work! Stop sponging of the state, "You don't see us millionaires and billionaires sitting with a cup on the street corners trying to make a pound or two".

So he flashed his smile to the cameras and 'commended this statement to the house' the Tories cheered and the Prime Minister shouted 'here here' and in a couple of days all that hot air will have floated up 'The Elizabeth Tower', past the bell 'Big Ben' and out through the restored clock face, which is known about the world, away up the sewage filled river Thames off into the sea to be forever forgotten.

Winnie Ewing

Time after time, on matters great and small, we
are still standing on the sidelines, mutely
accepting what is decided elsewhere instead of
raising our voices and making our own choices.
Scotland's much vaunted partnership of
Jonah and the whale.

Value
Social Media Post 2021

For many of my years I have promoted the idea of the value of people. The value of our planet, the animals, birds, trees and plants. When I write 'value' I am not thinking in terms of money. Keep numbers out of this argument.

Nature is natural, nothing in nature can be unnatural. Humans have spent centuries building 'cultures' and ever since culture has existed it has been at odds with nature.

Culture is everything that humans have constructed. Not just art, theatre and music. Numbers and money are parts of culture. Humans have taken these two tools and measured everything and everyone in Meters and Euros. It is easier than trying measure in 'nature'. The horror of facial recognition is down to measuring one point to another. Does it point out a value? No it does not. Does it show beauty? No it does not.

I have long thought that history leaves the story behind but in it's shadow is where we all live. In Scotland, in 1695, 1696, 1698 and 1699, many people will know, famine came upon Scottish people 'seven ill years'. Bitterly cold weather, failed harvest, trading barriers with France and problems trading cattle. The population of Scotland diminished by death and people leaving. 25% of people in Aberdeenshire perished.

The Battle of Culloden, 1746, was followed in 1750 by the start of the Highland Clearances, our people were forced of the land to make way for sheep and left Scotland for Nova Scotia, Ontario and the Carolinas.

On my travels in Europe, over many years, I met with and talked to many who had first hand knowledge of the Second World War. One of the things I have been told by many was of the memory of being invaded.

England and Scotland were bombed, many fine people lost their lives and how sad was it all. However they were not invaded. Which may show why many have never understood the European Union.

I would suggest that the shadow under which the English live is different from the shadow that we Scots live. Many Europeans live under the shadow of invasion. The English shadow has not those notes of invasion which continental Europeans feel or great population loss due to famine that Scots still feel.

The Westminster Government started collecting data on hunger only in 2019 and gave it's first report on that data in March 2021, so that great loss of people in the 1690's has cast a different shadow over us than the shadow cast over the English, who are currently in the shadows of 'glory days of empire' when they considered that they ruled the world.

Scots in general have a disposition, I think, that understands more deeply the value of our people. Adam Smith demonstrates how scarcity increases value. (Of course there are many fine English people who do understand value but that is not what I am writing about). In Scotland the value we see in others is demonstrated in such things as free prescriptions, free personal care, the huge programme that has built new and repaired over one thousand of our school buildings, the ten pounds a week child payment, the baby box, free meals for children. The huge uptake of the Covid vaccine. It is demonstrated every day, on the individual level, where people help one another.

Everything the Westminster Government does is about numbers and a lot of the numbers involve the question 'how much does it cost?' I often think they should look at things with the question 'how much will it cost if we do not do x y or z?'. There is always an opportunity cost i.e. if we did x then we could have done y or z.

The UK, as a whole, is haemorrhaging people right now. People have been laughing at a scheme set up to attract Nobel Laureate's to the UK. Whilst today there is a tragedy when desperate people drowned whilst trying to across the English Channel to get into England. Suddenly people are, sorry, and blaming anyone but themselves. For the 'valuable' lives lost.

The sadness is that many people fail to understand their own value, then they fail to understand the value of others, or indeed the value of anything. The value of people cannot be measured in money, weight, or length. Humans are natural, they are a part of nature, each is perfect. Culture can scream and shout all it wants that is the conundrum. Unless we all start to value one another via nature. Valuing each other via culture will surely bring the Homo Sapiens to an end.

There are to few truck drivers, to few night club bouncers and yet a flood of ingenious, hardy people, have travelled half way across the globe and are not frightened by 21 miles of grey sea water are apparently of less value than some other people.

The UK has many people who value only that which looks and sounds similar to themselves. Maybe it is only natural. I would say we really need a cultural shift which says we are all of value and we do not need rulers and calculators to work it out.

Scotland needs more self-help
and less self-flagulation

Also published in 'The National' 12 December 2021 2

Garbage in, garbage out' was said of computers back in the day. Jamie Oliver says it of children's school lunches in England. It is not only what folk choose to put in their stomachs, it is the garbage they let fall into their brains. I was writing about this in the 1990's, thirty years ago! I was not the only one. In his great book 'What to Say When You Talk To Your Self' Shad Helmstetter, writes that what we say to ourselves is so very important. Denis Waitley in his book 'The Psychology of Winning' writes about what Olympic Athletes say to themselves as they line up for the high jump. Do they say 'Oh my I am not sure about this', or do they say 'I have rehearsed this so many times, I am ready, I am going to do this'.

Susan Jeffers, in her great work, 'Feel the Fear and do it Anyway', says something similar, and gives a demonstrable example of what she means when anyone say's 'I am weak'. Read the book and you will find out. I do wish that people, in general, would catch up on their reading. Les Giblin, in 'Skill With People', writes, that those of us with the fortune of sight, learn 83% of what we know through our eyes. If I ruled the world these volumes would 'must reads' for everyone.

Video, probably from installed security cameras, in the £2.6 million pounds, 'Press Room' of 10 Downing Street, of Allegra Stratton, being coy in an a mock press briefing about parties, that took place in Downing Street last Christmas, which broke lock down regulations, have now been seen. The response is loud and clear. However it is Allegra who has to 'fall on her sword'. The world of Westminster politics grinds on with Johnson deflecting and redirecting all criticism, standing aloof and maintaining these sins were of his 'minions' not him. Unbelievably, to me, many seem to accept that.

Then I glance about the world and see the 'tin-pot-dictators' who now rule much of the political world. From the Philippines to Brazil, from Turkey to Australia, from Westminster to the Kremlin. I read the BBC, or should I more correctly write 'The English Broadcasting Corporation', report on Kate Forbes 's 'balanced budget' the Scottish financial statement 2021-2022….. Douglas Fraser wrote

'Big Vision, tight squeeze'. He went on to say:- *"That speech set out grand and uncontroversial themes: tackling inequality as it affects families and young people, helping Scotland make its contribution to reducing climate change and helping businesses recover from the pandemic. The last of these left businesses under-whelmed.*

It was not long ago that a 'super-majority' of Scottish voters gave their vote to Nicola Sturgeon to implement such policies. In the coming days, I predict Anas Sarwar (Scottish Labour

Leader) will tell Nicola Sturgeon that more money should be spent elsewhere and Douglas Ross (Scottish Tory Leader) will do the same. Nicola Sturgeon will then ask them both to tell her what cuts Kate Forbes should make in order that money can be spent elsewhere. We all know that they will not follow though with any sensible suggestions as they have none to offer. If they had Sarwar or Ross, would be at the helm. Thank goodness we have Nicola Sturgeon as First Minister.

Kate Forbes is correct to have a 'Big Vision', in her role as Finance Secretary she is speaking for Scotland, just like in the books I mentioned above, she is using good 'self-talk' and saying we, Scotland, are a strong and powerful nation, we can set out an ambitious plan, and we can achieve the goals which we set for ourselves.

The 'Tight Squeeze' Douglas Fraser invokes, is everything to do with the voters who coalesce around the likes of Johnson, and the other far-right politicians, who live, not by a vision of 'better for all', but by 'better for me and my mates'. The rest of the population are trained to put-up with what they get. After all the 'ordinaries' are 'ok' with what they have already got, and Westminster budgets are all about rewarding those who support the government and punishing those who do not.

Human-kind invented money, which means that human-kind could reinvent it so that all have plenty. It is not an outlandish thing to say, indeed *The National'* has provided 1000 Scot Coin to all subscribers, in the past few weeks, that is a reinvention of money. It is easy to see from the pandemic just how quickly change can be bought about. In China they built a 1500 bed hospital in 5 days. A vaccine against Covid was made in record time. Twenty months, or so ago the Government told entire the population to stay at home for months, and most of the people did as they were told.

When you set a goal - if you have a dead-line.... for example.... 'All these people will die by the end of the year so we need a vaccine now.' Magically, brilliant brains, search for the opportunities that are required to fulfil the dead-line. What disaster movie would be complete without the element of jeopardy - 'not enough time'? That is why the Greens and the SNP are right to call time on the Cambo oil field. Only when there is a dead-line do people pull out all the stops to find a solution. 'Oh heavens there is no coal, gas, or oil....Now what?' At that point, that is when humans open their eyes and see. Before that they cling to what they know, John F Kennedy put man on the moon because he set the goal.

The right wing gets support, for it is comfortable, it is what we know, we can spend our time tinkering about, refining what we already do, even though we know it killing us. No one knows the value of a fire-fighter until their house is burning down.

The 'Tight Squeeze', in Kate Forbes's budget, is due to all those who continue to vote for 'The Union', The Union that they think they know but that is something that disappeared, like the British Empire, long ago, and that the Johnson Mob still crave.

Those of us who vote for the SNP, and who will vote for Independence, have a vision for Scotland with full control over our financial situation, with our own central bank, where budgets are used to create money to reward everyone in our country and spur them on to even better.

Our forefather Scots 'Enlightened the World' in the 18th century. The Union with rUK now stifles and holds us back. We need to 'Feel the Fear and do it Anyway', We must tell ourselves 'We are big enough, rich enough, strong enough'. We reject the 'tin-pot dictatorships' and the garbage propaganda of the EBC. We know how to talk to ourselves. We have 'Big Visions' and we can see a better future for all the citizens of our wonderful, free and Independent country. Read this again 'Good stuff in, Good stuff out'.

Cher Bonfis

The Opportunity Cost is Life or Death Rishi
Social Media Post 2021

Adam Smith (1723-1790) a great figure in the 'Scottish Enlightenment'. He wrote 'The Wealth of Nations' a book which still effects the lives of every Scot. Maynard Keynes gave us Macro-Economics. We are all bound to these theories and our money is still under the influence of the 'moral fortitude' of the times of Mary Queen of Scots, when John Knox bought the reformation ideas of Calvin, from Geneva. All those moral obligations to be debt free or get your ear lobe nailed to the Tron.

In Kirkcaldy is 'The Adam Smith Theatre'. Economics is a theatre. Shakespeare wrote 'All the worlds a stage'. Remember it was Shakespeare who undermined our King MacBeth, Son of Life. A King who understood the value of people. The value of people is sometimes misunderstood. Numbers are easily understood, or are they? 1 + 1 = 2. Now hold your index fingers and bring them together so that there is a small space between them, now you have 11. Numbers are tricky things. Can/do they give us value?

James Carville made up a phrase for Bill Clinton's US Presidential campaign 1992. 'The economy, stupid'. The anchor of elections is the economy.

Somewhere, deep in our reptilian brain, are echoes of Smith and Keynes and Knox. If you do a favour for a Scottish pal they will wish to square you up, balance the books, return the favour. In Switzerland too, 'never be in anyone else's pocket, be independent'.

You and me, our businesses, our work to produce goods and services, our savings and our debts are what makes up the Scottish economy. It is the theatre in which to act and to date it is the best human kind has invented. For despite the anomalies of some people having far too much and others having far to little. For the main part huge numbers of people have enough to survive and there are many who get to have a very reasonable time of it.

The pandemic was as an earthquake, there was a sudden feeling of insecurity and the cold wind of terror as people wondered how to pay their bills. The word was 'uncertainty'. Of course life is never certain but people got very worried. Things worked out for many people during the first lockdown. Money came from those who often seem to consider themselves as our 'betters' in 11 Downing Street. Now we come to the next bump in this pandemic and there seems to be less willingness on the part of Sunak to pump in some more cash. Rishi there will be more bumps and completely different bumps, there are always bumps.

The answer to your question, which is 'why is there less willingness?' I will try to explain

Adam Smith wrote about the manufacture of a pin.

The Division of Labour:- One worker does this, another worker does that. People specialise, they acquire knowledge and skills in a particular area, it can make them less mobile in the work force, but the quality of that which they produce is very good.

Supply and Demand:- A market consists of buyers and sellers. If a seller has 10 boxes of chocolates and 20 people want to buy the seller can raise/inflate the price until 10 people decide that the chocolates are not worth it and they drop out of the market. If the market trader has 10 boxes of chocolates but prospective buyers think that the price is to high the trader can lower the price until 10 people think that that the lower price is worth it.

Where supply and demand meet is the price, or the value, given to the product, or service. People say, falsely, that their house, their car, their painting worth such and such. In economics the only time any product, or service, has a monetary value is at the point of sale, the fleeting moment when the coins/notes meet the sellers palm, or bank account. Things may have a utilitarian value, the house may keep you from the rain, but that is not value in economics.

Inflation:- If a lot of people wish to buy but the quantity of goods for sale is limited prices will rise.

Opportunity Cost:- If you have a fixed amount of money, and the things you need to buy exceed that amount, choices must be made. Buy this and not that. The opportunity to buy this means that the cost in taking that opportunity is not to buy the other, this is measured buy the value/price of the item you did not purchase.

Governments are again in Pandemic panic mode. They have few weapons available; limiting peoples interactions is effective. If people are to stay away from work financial support is required. Our Scottish Government view is that our people have an intrinsic value beyond economics. Nicola Sturgeon will tell you that her first responsibility is to keep people safe. Well the first responsibility of any Government is to protect it's people. Which is why we have armed forces. Unfortunately those powers reside in England. The finance for Scotland resides in England. So when Kate Forbes needs to find extra cash, without support of the UK treasury, she must look at the 'Opportunity Cost' 'if I do this I cannot do that'. Rishi Sunak has the Bank of England, which allows the creation of as much cash as is required at any time. So he really does not need to get involved with opportunity cost, (with the caveat printed below). The Pandemic has been going on for fewer than two years. World War Two took five years. They found money for bombs, they always find money for bombs, borrowing money in the 1939-1945 era was much more difficult than it is today.

The difficult situation arising now is because of Brexit. Johnson loves to hide behind the smoke screen of the Pandemic but it is Brexit that is the problem. Brexit has caused a slow down in the supply of commodities and this is due to be worse in 2022 when import restrictions come into force. Goods and Services are in short supply. Yet there is a lot of money around because there have been loans and furlough, etc. 'Too much money chasing too few goods' equals inflation.

There are also fewer workers because many EU citizens left the UK. The market place for workers is also corrupted by the UK Government immigration policy, again something controlled by England, so the price of labour rises. Andrew Bailey is, right now, worried, he is probably looking back at Adam Smith and Maynard Keynes saying to himself as he climbs out of bed in the morning, 'too much money chasing to few goods'. The Bank of England are supposed to keep inflation at 2% (In my memory Keynes said 4% is good as it motivates people to do better. Something about if you have a $400 you don't want the $200 suit any more). Shadows of the 1930's creep out of dusty cupboards in 11 Downing Street, and the phrase 'morally ethical' is whispered. There lurks the memory of Hitler's rise and 'hyper-inflation', we don't want that again. Economics is not really about morals, it is about numbers. Adam did write 'The Theory of Moral Sentiments' - but more of that another time.

Rishi, is now faced with an 'Opportunity Cost' scenario, which is moral issue of life and death. If he does not provide funding to help people stay away from work and for businesses to, again, be in suspended animation. People will continue to interact, the virus will spread and more people will die. So Rishi Inflation or death? Your opportunity cost tonight.

We need to overhaul the whole financial system, it cannot be right that there are 20, or so, billionaires with more wealth than everybody else on the planet and some people have no proper water supply or toilets and people have to sleep on the streets in Glasgow.

For us Scots the first step along that road is to become Independent and gain control of that which England currently controls. The First Minister we elect will want to protect us, for their position relies upon our votes. Currently Scots who vote Tory are thin on the ground and so their votes in Tory-Land Westminster, these votes may completely disappear at the next election, so they are not really worth much to *Johnson* so why would Johnson loose sleep over Scottish voters, after all he thinks that *'Murray Ross'* is the leader of the Scottish Conservatives (I bet he would spell it like that), if you look back over his comments about us Scots it is hard to think that he would not.

We can only really be safe when the rest of humanity is safe. Unfortunately a devolved administration has not enough power to even start dealing with that idea. Imagine if we spent money on making humanity as a whole watered, fed and safe. Instead of enriching arms dealers to, maybe, keep a few of us, the rich, safe.

There it is again the Opportunity Cost.

RT Tunstall

Scotland has a built-in sound system
that never stops thumping.

Hugh MacDiarmid

It is time we in Scotland put England in its
proper place and instead of our leaning on
England and taking inspiration from her, we
should lean and turn to Europe, for it is there
our future prosperity lies.

Here's where the focus should lie
in our quest for independence

Also published in 'The National' 28 December 2021 3

Amongst those of us who have longed for, fought for, marched for, stuffed leaflets for, contributed funds for. There are those who are impatient and those who are super-impatient for Independence. Whenever the Herald announced a split in the SNP I often thought well the fault line described is not actually what I see. Then Alex Salmond stepped up with his 'Alba Party', it seemed to me, that many of the 'Super Impatient' of the SNP slipped away and became members of Alba. There was talk of mastering the 'List Vote' and causing a 'Super Majority', in Holyrood, for Independence.

I thought of the fall of the Berlin Wall and how the power of the people, with single minded purpose, bought that monstrosity to an end. Then my thought was, that if we are really serious about Independence, we need to be as a welding torch or a laser beam, all of us working together for the same ends, white hot focus. Marching until the walls come tumbling down, rather than defragmenting into multiple groups as 'The All Under One Banner' crowd have done.

If we are going to get our Independence it will be less easily achieved by internal fights. I would say that it will require all of us, who want it, to direct all our energy to helping the doubters and the staunch Unionists that the people, who are Scotland, will be better off in every way, in a small Independent country. Every moment wasted in moaning amongst ourselves is a moment, that could have been used better to help the undecided move to a position that is favourable to a Yes response in the next Independence Referendum.

The SNP have spent 88 years building and making the party. It may take Alba a longer or a shorter time to reach a similar position on the political landscape. However the idea that a surprise dash for list votes, few moments before an election, was a confusion for many ordinary voters, many of whom really do not get the idea of the 2 votes and what the second of their votes will achieve, or not achieve, in their area. My neighbour dislikes Nicola Sturgeon, she told me therefore she would vote Tory. I said to her that in this area, if her idea was to get rid of Nicola Sturgeon, her best bet was to give her votes to Labour. As much as I tried to explain she did not grasp what I had tried to get her to understand.

My neighbour is not a supporter of Nicola Sturgeon. I am and I think that there are some things that really need to be put straight. I read that some people think that she is not really interested in Scottish Independence, I read that some think that is because she likes the power of being First Minister. Some say it is her fault that we have not had a second shot at a referendum or that it is her fault that she has not march up Downing Street with a copy of the Declaration of Arbroath and told Boris Johnson to put the Union where the sun cannot shine.

Really? Come on, again this is time wasting. I am sure some of you will come back at me and tell me the contrary but before you get all upset think on these.

Rhodesia was an unrecognised state for fourteen years after the Unilateral Declaration of Independence. Which means it was not Independent at all. Unless other countries agree that your nation is an independent country it is nothing. Currently the Secretary of State for Defence is a position held for all of the United Kingdom by the UK Government. Scotland has no armed forces to protect and defend it, other than the forces loyal to Her Majesty Queen Elizabeth and controlled by the Westminster Government. We can shout and scream for Independence but with no force capable for securing such, what will we be able to do? Look at the 'mental' force used by the Spanish over Catalonia. Look at the Chinese take over in Hong Kong. In this day and age would there be Scottish 'Freedom Fighters' who would over run the 'Central Post Office' as in 1920's Ireland? Would there be a Scottish 'Mau Mau' as 1952 to 1960 in Kenya? I do not think that that is what Scottish people do. I would not want them to do that either. It is not the way. Besides death, and destruction, and the endless bitterness, that such would cause is a price I do not think Scotland is willing to pay. Peace and good will towards all, after all it is that time of year, that is the Scottish way.

The way to Independence is to have a majority of Scottish citizens to vote for it. In sufficient numbers that our children and their children can be so proud of their nation that they will defend it with their hearts, and minds.

So my appeal to you is this:- If you want Scotland to be an Independent country start making conversations with all who you meet, family, friends and strangers. Listen to them and find out what they think. Keep your mouth shut, they will already know what you think. Keep asking them why they think what they think. Inform yourself and understand that the reason someone does not want Independence it is because they fear the unknown....... Take away their fears.

Scotland will not become an Independent Nation without the SNP. Currently Nicola Sturgeon is the leader of the party. One day she will decide that she wants to do other things. For now if you doubt her, for one moment, you really are missing the point and you really do not understand her or what we are trying to do. She is showing that Scotland can put on a better show than can the UK as a whole. That is the message it is your responsibility to deliver, to as many people as you can.

Our Independence is really up to you.

Indyref2 date isn't required before we engage No voters in conversation

Also published in 'The National' 03 January 2022 4

Feelings. There is so much I do not understand about the world, indeed the universe. A neighbour and his son stopped by with late Christmas Greetings and early Hogmanay thoughts. "Lang Ma Yer Lum Reek" he smiled and his thirteen year old boy asked "What did you just say?" I like these two people we often blether and the Faither often lights up his vocabulary with Scots words from here. It will be a braw day and a mawkit mogger that he had to deal with at his work last week. He has only the yin son and as I questioned it became apparent that much of the vocabulary floated around and over the boy's ears, never heard. Instead his mind was full of a new 'virtual reality' set he had been given for Christmas, this will take him right into worlds which I will never inhabit. Of course that is the way of things, generation changes to generation, the infrastructure around folks alters and so the systems used to communicate change. I tried to speak of Rabbie Burns and 'Ault Lang Syne' but the response from the boy was "Oh look at that spider". I thought it best not to follow through with a reference to Robert the Bruce. Now of course there could be many a tale you can fussle up to counter the above, at least I really hope you can. My feeling is that there will be many a similar tale to be told.

Another thing that I find so difficult to grasp is folk who want to see a referendum on our Independence given a solid date in the future, before they feel they can be motivated to do something about promoting Independence. In deed why do we need a date? When there are still so many to convert to the cause. Independence is a journey not a destination. I feel that that is an awkward phrase but even when we have achieved Independence we will still be on that journey of creating an up-dated version of our great and wonderful country. Maybe that is the point I was missing in the first paragraph, as I am gey depressed to hear expressions like 'gonna' I have to accept many people use this, just as they now start sentences with BUT, or AND, of BECAUSE, even though I feel they should not.

When we do get a date, most likely a day around eighteen months from now, that will ignite the blue touch paper but in the meantime any of us who want Independence are already using the time to promote the cause. Have you ever noticed how every day products are continually advertised, fizzy drinks, chocolate bars, whatever. If I write 'Fork Lift Truck'... now what are you thinking of? We need Independence to be on the lips and in the minds of the majority of Scottish people. Believe it or not, many rarely think about it, they are busy in their own virtual reality. They have a whole heap of emotions and feelings to deal with every day, many of which have a much higher priority in their lives.

Whilst it may well help to have a brain full of answers to questions, (*The National* publishes many 'door step responses' under 'Fact Check'. Also *'Scotland The Brief'* by Gordon MacIntyre-Kemp), the best plan of action, I have seen, requires no money or leaflets, it merely requires conversation.

The important thing is to pose questions to the doubters, the unionists and those who would vote no or not at all. Question and listen, then question the answers they give. No one needs to be a genius to do this, those of us who do this do it with friends, family and strangers, it can take a moment or a long time. Once practised it can be done at anytime, anywhere, with just about anyone you meet. None of us need a referendum date to start to do this. It can be done face to face, or on the phone, by email or a text message. It could start, for example, "In the light of all that has gone on in Westminster this past year what are your thoughts now about an Independent Scotland?" We listen and compliment "What you say is interesting". There is no point in contradicting, there is no point in arguing, instead ask for more detail and question "Why do you say that?" Keep asking questions. Remember that all the logic in the world is less likely to help a person to yes than when they find the emotion. It is emotion that motivates us and that is an internal force, which can not be strapped on from the outside. Ultimately it is how we will all feel in our newly Independent Nation. So as Morris Albert sang, forty seven years ago "Feelings nothing more than feelings." Lang Ma Yer Lum Reek.

Cher Bonfis

Devo-max: By Jingo,
let's cease the talk of this old chestnut

Also published in 'The National' 08 January 2022 5

I had a teacher at school and when he got really cross he would say 'By Jingo!' 'By Jingo!' could be interpreted as a positive, confirming the truth, or importance of something, however from the tone in my teachers voice it was obviously an expression of his anger about some misdemeanour or another.

When I saw the front page of *The National'* last night, before I went to bed, 'BY JINGO!' is what flooded my head. I lay awake trying to remember how many times I have marched through Perth, Inverness, Oban, Campeltown, Glasgow, Edinburgh, Dumfries. How much effort it took me to get to these places, how much money it cost in fares and over-night stays. I tried, in my head, to calculate how many donations I have made to various parts of the YES movement and the SNP. How many letters I have written to *The National'.* How many times people have disagreed and agreed with me in articles on social media. How many people I have spoken to who have not been persuaded by my logic, emotion or enthusiasm. I thought of many of my companions, I ran through their faces through my head and knew that in their eyes what they wanted was the same as that which I want an Independent Scotland.

I know that they, as have I, have that one dream in mind. So to see the old chestnut of devo-max splashed all over 'The National's' front page. Worse still Chris Hanlon reminding people of it.

For goodness sake words fail me and I find myself shaking and pulsating, I would probably be assigned to an anger management programme if anyone could see me right now.

We are all surely aware that 'The Vow' meant absolutely nothing. Surely people who are reading this can see how the current Westminster Government undermine our Holyrood Parliament with their 'Internal Market' Legislation. Chris Halon suggesting that Boris Johnson would be more amenable to a Section 30 if this was apart of deal makes me feel like crying.

Just recently, ok I know the Pandemic gave it a lift, YES polled at over 60%. We know how Tommy Sheppard has fought to gain access to the results of secret polling, carried out by the UK Government on Independence, and how despite courts telling Gove that the information should be made public, Johnson and his ministers are terrified to publish.

We still live in a democracy, so I have to live, now, in this strange thing called the United Kingdom. I look to Holyrood and admire the pioneering legislation The Child Payment and the Baby Box. I see the Westminster Parliament over-riding legislation which was to incorporate the United Nations Laws on the Rights of Children into Scots Law. We hear of desperate conditions that refugees are forced to endure and even the deaths of some whilst in the care of the UK Government. I read a press release which notes that on average Scottish people pay eight hundreds and forty fewer pounds in taxes and statutory charges than do people in England each year. Whilst one million Scottish pensioners will have two-thousand-six-hundred fewer pounds to spend over the next five years because the triple lock on pensions has been scraped by the UK Governement. UK pensions are very low by the standards of many other countries already. We see the UK Government increase the stock pile of useless nuclear weapons as they commission the building of a new Royal Yacht, whilst swimming in a sea of corruption.

We still live in a democracy, for how much longer? Who knows? A quick glance at some history books, or even a look at some films on the subject's of Communism, or Fascism is enough to scare me when I look around the world and to the south of our Scottish Border.

Here in Scotland the majority have voted SNP time and time again and that is the message that needs to be heard, so we must be louder, obviously, for we still need to make it plain. Not to sully the conversation with third options, which will only result in confusing the many who take little interest in all of this, the very people we need to increase the number who will vote to make Scotland Independent. One clear dream Independence, nothing less. 'By Jingo!'

My ears must have deceived me on Douglas Ross interview

Also published in 'The National' 16 January 2022 6

Bermans & Nathams, film costumiers in London is a spectacular place to visit. I do not think they do tours, so it is unlikely you can get a ticket. Back in the day, when I had involvement in television productions, I received an invitation to visit. It really was a place that could take your brain into an actual history. It was a huge building on several floors and at the end of the visit so mesmerised was I, I climbed into the lift and for some moments forgot where I really was.

The lift stuttered to a halt, the door slid open and there standing before me was a Officer from World War II Germany! Just for a second I actually thought I had been in Doctor Who's Tardis, (A few days before I had shared another lift with Tom Baker and Mary Tamm) so it was in my head I suppose and I really did think I had landed somewhere in 1943. I emerged from this hallucination because I recognised the actor, we greeted one another and he had a good laugh at me when I told him this story.

Yesterday was a kind of similar experience. I watched Colin MacKay, of *STV news*, interviewing Douglas Ross and I thought that I heard Douglas Ross say that Prime Minister, Boris Johnson, should resign! I shook my head from side to side, I checked the internet and found myself again in the lift shaft Tardis at *Bemmans & Nathams*, for in this particular work by Salvador Dali the clocks were dripping all over the place and for the first time in my life I found myself in agreement with a Tory! Someone, no less, than the 'Leader' of the Conservatives of Scotland! If that is not surreal, what is?

I pealed the wrapper from a 'Chuppa Cups' and sucked as I contemplated. (NB: Salvador designed the 'Chuppa Cups' logo).

The next thing I was aware of was criticism of Douglas Ross by Michael-Aberdeen-Gove and Jacob-Central Fife-Rees-Mogg. Claiming that *'Murray Ross',* as Boris Johnson calls him, (Come-on! Johnson's knowledge of 'Moray' will be that that is where the great waving fields of butter mints are grown, because the temperate climate along the strath of the river Spey) was nothing but a 'light weight' in the Conservative and Unionist Party. The River Spey? That's in North Britain, somewhere, according to the MI6 version of the CIA's 'World Fact Book'.

Then I thought....'Am I being taken for a sucker?' Is this an elaborate ploy by some person who works in Tory Party Central? We know that Johnson really cares nothing about what is said about him. Good, bad or ugly as long as his picture is on the front of the newspaper that is good enough for him. So is this a way of upping the profile of Douglas Ross? My neighbour voted Tory but she would not know Douglas Ross from a butter mint. So here, on a day when Sir. John Curtis said that the Tories are polling at only 17% in Scotland, which is the lowest since the Jurassic period, Douglas gets more media exposure than he has ever had and Boris gets a bit more, because two Tory grandees shower Ross with insults. Douglas is used to insults as football supporters often shout at referees suggesting they should at least clean their spectacles before a match begins.

I climbed out of the Tardis again and realised that a flash of sympathy had passed through my cerebral cortex for a man for whom I had previously only felt distain. It echoed in my ear 'poor Douglas', even his 'betters' dislike him. Then I thought could there be anyone in the Tory Party with that much aforethought, to plot to increase Ross's notoriety, in such a devious fashion? Then it struck me that it was a Tory official who invited a hundred people to a work meeting - sorry party - and to bring their own booze, during 'Lock-Down-One', (Now there is a title for a TV series).

Before Ruth Davidson put on her ermine I did send here a letter, I suggested that when Scotland is Independent, she could throw her hat in the ring and have at least a chance of becoming the First Minister of a whole country. Whilst, at that time, there was little chance of her becoming the Prime Minister of the disunited Kingdom. I asked why would she no support IndyRef2 with that idea in mind. If she saw that letter I am sure she would have laughed. I expect an advisor filed my missive in the wasted paper bin before it got to Ruth's desk. If she had written back to me, to congratulate me for the suggestion, an idea she had not thought of, it would have been truly surreal. Yet I wonder now, after this minor earthquake, if the Tory MSP's are having similar thoughts, because if Murray Ross has a chance of being big chief in Scotland, there might be a slightly better opportunity to advance their own career! In their minds, right now, maybe the status of Scotland as a regional out-post of Tory England might be changing to an image of an Independent Country, where they might, one day, actually have a chance to be king of the castle…...Oh sorry what kind of Salvador Dali, nightmare painting was I in just then?

"Has nay one got a butter mint? I have woken up with a really bad taste in my mouth....Yes fine a 'Chuppa Cups' will do the trick. Thank you. Yes I am calling Colin MacKay, for I must really check that Douglas Ross did say that, and that Gove and Mogg said that, and even more, hilariously, I sure I heard Mogg say that Alistair Jack is a big figure in Scottish politics!

Benefits of independent Scotland investing in clean water are crystal clear

Also published in 'The National' 30 January 2022 7

In my computer there are 23486 photographs. When I have finished writing something there is a new memory on the screen - my children, a picture of Spey-side or something else. This morning the wood-shed of my house in Banffshire. A pile of whisky barrel off cuts to burn warm on winter nights at that wee bothy. That place has a private water supply, crystal clear Scottish water. In the photo was a wheelbarrow. I wondered just how many wheelbarrows I have owned in my life? I like these kinds of questions they make me delve into memory banks I seldom access and give me assurance that, fortunately, dementia has not yet a grip. I do notice lack of memory in the mass media though, it frequently worries me. Stories sometimes on the same day even the same bulletin, which completely contradict one another and with no link to reports only the evening before. I expect that Prime Minister Johnson is happy with this.

Keeping up with the news is hard, there is so much. One major source of news is the BBC. In Scotland we often call it the English Broadcasting Corporation, that be as in may, there are many fine people who work for it and they do provide so much that is worthy. I will confess to having received payments, for services rendered, in former times, from it.

I would criticise the BBC news website as it uses many photographs which appear to be staged, some look like studio shots for the cover of a glossy magazine. People like Taylor Swift manage to get themselves stories, usually around the time of their up coming tour or new album. I suppose many folk must want it like that. I am an old fashioned misery guts wishing the likes of William Hardcastle, Derek Cooper, and Fyfe Robinson were still about, at least serious things were serious then. Now they add background music, as in a Hollywood movie, when presenting important information. Sometimes it seems reporters and editors have absolutely no memory of previous stories. Many items are presented as stand-alone.

Today I tried to watch a video 'No average Joe: President Biden's first year in four minutes'. This was a montage to far for me. Then I clicked for a video 'Giant pristine coral reef discovered off Tahiti', I thought 'Why tell everybody?' Now there will be cruise ships full of scuba diving tourists messing it all up! The next video was 'Sewage found in UK rivers', I thought is that a surprise? There have been lots of similar stories recently. I saw a man peer into a computer screen, it displayed a video from an underwater camera, he described the mawkit water (they put music in the back ground of this video too). A caption provided information that on 3100 days, over the past 4 years, sewage has been illegally dumped in English rivers! There are only 1461 days in 4 years!

The video made no mention of 07 September 2021 when the Environment Agency gave polluters permission to dump raw effluent as the supply of chemicals to clean the sewage had been disrupted by Brexit. No mention that 'Water Companies: Sewage Discharge' was debated in Westminster 15 November 2021 following e-petition 582336. The UK Government's response to that was that water companies would make real time data available so that swimmers and surfers would know when to expect the next tsunami of wet wipes, faeces and sanitary products. Water companies in England are private enterprises. In my opinion the private sector working at it's most disgusting, base, level. How could it be that organisations where the first motivation is to make a profit could be in charge of the second most important thing that sustains life. In many places water rights have been purchased by private companies. I remember 17 years ago being involved in a petition against allowing a multinational soft-drinks manufacturer to buy the rights to water along the Bodensee that straddles Germany and Switzerland. The *sees* (lochs) of Switzerland are clean and available for swimming, the Swiss have dedicated police to enforce strict environmental controls appertaining to their water ways. I wish Scotland had such a force.

Scotland's water belongs to us via Scottish Water. Sometimes it too discharges sewage into Scottish rivers through 3697 combined sewer overflows, these operate as an emergency back-up system if flash flooding overwhelms urban sewer systems. Fines have been levied over discharges into the

Clyde. Scottish Water invests 40% of it's annual budget on capital projects, that is about £600 million, and another £170 million per year on servicing PFI debts, (PFI - Private Finance Intiatives were a John Major plan scooped up by Tony Blair to get private companies to invest in public projects they have mostly turned into financial millstones for the NHS and Education - so much so that Tory Chancellor Philip Hammond scrapped the idea of using them in the future – we are all still paying the legacy and will do so for many years to come). The money spent servicing PFI could otherwise be invested in new infrastructure. There are voices who would suggest Scotland lags behind the rUK on clean water issues I do not have information to make a judgment, I am not suggesting any of this is easy but given a choice between swimming in the Thames or the Spey I would not choose the Thames. Many of the problems can be traced back to disastrous acts of the Thatcher administration. (Don't get me started).

I repeat to put basic, life sustaining, human requirements, into the hands of businesses, whose sole aim is to make profit for shareholders. What kind of idea is that? Yet we allow business to pollute the air we breath as well. We need air above water and water above food. You could counter my argument by telling me that food is in the hands of business and then shelter and clothing would follow. The human comfort zone for warmth about 15 to 25 degrees and there are challenges below and above these figures which need defence, therefore clothes and food are above guns and bombs.

On 25 October 2021 Tory MP's voted for a an amendment to the Environment Bill which placed no legal obligation on water companies not to dump sewage into rivers in England. PFI is a scandal which now sucks much of the annual budgets from these projects, into the coffers of private corporations.

I am sure stand-alone stories where links between different happenings are not apparent are useful to the UK Government. Boris Johnson avoids answering questions by saying "Oh well but what people are really interested in is ...." deflecting and confusing. Making it even more difficult to remember what happened and when. He does this in every interview. He also knows that enquiries take time and that time is best filled with as many distracting stories as possible, making the sewage filled waters even cloudier.

Investment in infrastructure, to replace those sewer overflows, could be one of the great benefits of our new Independent Scotland. In younger times the Gillie's would chase us if they caught us swimming in the Spey. My memories are crystal clear.

Cher Bonfis

We should be glad to have our FM, and also her able deputy

Also published in 'The National' 31 January 2022 8

We Scots have so much to be thankful for. There are some who will disagree with what I will write, but surely even the strongest Labour, Lib Dem, or even Tory must feel some sense of, at the very least, 'uncomfortableness', around the sleaze of Party-Gate. Not to mention all the other provocative Ten Downing Street happenings during the entire time of it's present occupancy.

Matt Hancock kissing in full view of CCTV cameras. Allegra Stratton's 'mock the press' conference. Dominick Cummings testing his ability to see clearly whilst driving on the public highway. Extraordinary amounts of money spent on decorations for the flat above number eleven Downing Street. Liz Truss spending half a million pounds to fly her 14 person team to Australia, even at £3000 return per person, which would be an expensive fare, that would have been *only* £42000.

There are currently 359 Conservative MP's in the Westminster Parliament, 86 of those are women. To trigger a leadership contest 54 of these have to send a letter to Sir Graham Brady saying that they no longer have confidence in Boris Johnson.

Yet, despite the Metropolitan Polis announcement on an investigation into Party-Gate and Sue Gray's report there are not 54 people, in the parliamentary Conservative group of MP's, who are willing to write letters.

It makes me wonder what sort of hold Johnson's whips have on those three hundred and fifty nine MP's, what a back catalogue of misdemeanour and blackmail that must be! Or are they all expecting Johnson to make good on whatever wild promise he has made to them or is it just the terror of loosing such a vast MP's salary? These people scarily have huge effect on all our Scottish lives.

In all that group, commentators suggest, that the front runners to replace Boris Johnson would be Rishi Sunak and Liz Truss...out of 359! That is the choice?

By wonderful contrast, here in our Scottish Politics, we know that on the night before it was found that Nicola Sturgeon had not broken the Ministerial Code, she had spoken with John Swinney and said to him that he should be prepared to take over as First Minister should things not go in her favour.

I think we are extremely fortunate to have Nicola Sturgeon as our First Minister she has a proper command of what it takes to be a leader. I want her to stay on as First Minister for many years to come.

If things had gone wrong though we all know that John Swinney would have had no difficulty in stepping up and doing a fine Job. Indeed there are many in the upper ranks of the SNP who could take on and make great success of the role. I am sure too that if a First Minister of Scotland were to do a fraction of the things that have been reported from the Westminster Parliament, our MSP's would not be quiet about it.

Nicola Sturgeon has information at hand to respond to questions and she does, frequently providing context and often in much more detail than the questioner had been expecting. In contrast Johnson usually dismisses questions by saying that people are not interested in the answer but they are interested in..... at which point he blurts out his sound bite of the day.

We have a lot to be thankful for in Scotland but the dead weight of London rule is a shoddy encumbrance upon our nation and the high values that most of us aspire to. As the next referendum comes economic matters will come up as the 'most important' of issues during debates. I hope that people will see beyond the money. Scotland is rich and capable, the economics will take care of themselves, numbers are the easy bit. For me it is Independence for a better life for our people, that does not necessarily have anything to do with money. It is about decent living, compassion, and kindness. A set of values and code of conduct to live by. It is about being able to shout out loud and clear, that we are proud and happy to

be Independent Scots who have so much to offer and so
much more to be thankful for.

George Bernard Shaw

Liberty Requires responsibility
that is why most men dread it

Albert Camnus

Freedom is nothing else
than a chance to be better

Terry Pratchett's books helped me see how Boris Johnson functions

Also published in 'The National' 06 February 2022 9

Terry Pratchett, for me a beacon through the mirk and haar of life. I often think our world and Terry's 'Disk-World' have collided. Last week these classic works were in the news, Jack Munroe was given permission, from Terry Pratchett's estate, to use 'Vimes Boots Index' to high-light the current high inflation rates. The 'Disk-World' is, to me, a distorted version of our world, it has helped me understand this world more clearly and from the book "Small Gods" there was so much I understood.

Johnson wants a high income economy. Few would go against that but in economics, as in life, where there is a Yin there has to be a Yang.

The current Westminster Government seems to understand economics in simple terms i.e. in a 'Perfect Market' where all the buyers and sellers have full knowledge of each other and of all the available products/services. Labour, that is the workers, can move freely from job to any job. These ideas may sound simple but are a very tall order in reality.

In reality markets are always distorted by Government policy, subsidies, knowledge etc. Labour is seldom able to flit from any job to any job. Doctors, for example, have to be trained and they have to pass examinations before they are allowed to transplant hearts. Drivers of heavy goods vehicles must also be qualified. The requirement for qualification distorts a 'Perfect Market' as HGV drivers cannot move freely from driving lorries to heart surgery. Currently there are not enough qualified workers, in particular areas. That is where one of the wheels falls off of the Tory bus.

The current strategy involves the idea of supply and demand. Reduce the supply of labour whilst demand remains the same or rises and the price of labour rises. Companies compete by paying more, to attract and retain staff. In simple economics terms that idea should work, however in order to pay higher wages companies generally increase the price of the goods/services they sell or they risk unhappy stock holders if dividends are reduced. Rising prices in the shops is inflation and the amount of goods/services that can be purchased from a given amount reduces. Anomalies will also occur because those employed by the government or local government seldom achieve the wage rates paid in the private sector.

Brexit has not only restricted exports into the EU but imports to the UK as well. Whilst businesses desperately try to change all they have been doing over the past forty years shortages in supplies of imported goods from Europe add to the inflation spiral. Price is determined where supply and demand meet. Limit the supply and the price rises. Governments can increase and decease prices by taxing various products, VAT, Stamp Duty, Fuel Duty etc. So we do not operate in 'Perfect Markets'. That is surely easily understood.

PB

Terry Prachett books have helped me see clearly how we humans function here on our little planet. His book 'Small Gods' shows how we humans create and use our 'gods'. Kings/Queens, have evoked 'god' to bend populations to their will. Religion is a perfectly good concept and many religions bring comfort and understanding and a code to live by. In former times they were the foundations of society. The negative side of religion is seen when sectarian violence erupts or one religious group claims superiority over another. My interest in writing this today is that David Davis invoked 'God' to try and make Johnson resign and Michael Gove evoked 'god' to save Johnson from 'Party Gate'.

Kings/Queens are just human beings, in reality they have no super human powers, they cannot avoid cancer, divorce, criminal prosecution, like the rest of us when it snows they feel cold. So when Kings/Queens wanted people to do things that people do not want to do, the King/Queen said well if you choose not to do what I want you to do 'god' will be angry. Nobody can prove or disprove the existence of 'God' so the King/Queen has power. He/she is anointed 'god' on earth. Indeed James VI of Scotland/who was also King James I of England, 1566 to 1625, pushed the idea of the 'Divine Right of Kings' all the way up the hill and was often times un-iked. They cried him 'The Scotch Monkey', with his over sized head and ginger hair.

Surely there is no one on earth who would think of David Davis or Michael Gove as kings or gods! Maybe the Prime Minister has aspirations in that direction. There are those who might riley question if these people have any 'right' at all! For all that, a man's a man for all that but heavens, the journalist Andrew Neil and Michael Gove were together on a TV show last evening and Michael Gove said "I'm sure that when the report (Sue Gray's report into the parties at number ten) is published there will be from individuals concerned recognition, contrition and so on, and you know we owe them an element of Christian forgiveness."

Well there it is again, the 'elite' lording it over the everyday folk and using Religion/Christianity/'God' to defend the indefensible, to try and save the political life of 'King Boris' as marches off to Ukraine looking for a wee bit war, in the hope that he might get a bounce in the polls as did the Tory goddess Thatcher from the Falklands war.

Economics misunderstood, religion misunderstood, lock-down rules misunderstood? Thousands of people grieving the loss of mothers, fathers, sons, daughters, friends and colleagues, and still the Tory Government understands nothing but a craving for power. Even with all this there are still Scots who have not yet understood our need and right to be Independent.

Terry Pratchett.

"It's not worth doing something unless someone, somewhere, would much rather you weren't doing it." –

Margo MacDonald

When I am in the Scottish Parliament chamber, I often feel the need to sit for the entire debate. It's only courteous to listen to what everyone has to say, although I often find myself desperate to say something but too scared to stand up in case I regret it.

The UK Government is trampling
over Scotland again with freeports
Also published in 'The National' 16 February 2022 10

EVERY day it is just another damn thing. So what do you think of "freeports"? For my money if it has any thing to do with the Tories and Boris Johnson, what the heck are we doing even to consider it? Johnson says it will level us up, or will it just give 2 areas of Scotland a bit of an advantage? Levelling them up and the rest down?

The European Union does not think "free economic zones", as they are also known, are such a fine idea; since the UK left the EU they have been clamping down on 82 "free zones". They found that the special status of such areas had aided the financing of terrorism, money-laundering and organised crime.

In international terms they are supposed to simplify and harmonise customs procedures, which I find ironic as the Westminster government's outstanding achievement with Brexit is to make trading between the UK and the continent of Europe, and the UK, mainland, and Northern Ireland, so complex that many exporters and importers have given up.

You may be conversant with the term "Cinque Ports". These were/are a group of towns in Kent and Sussex in England.

Hastings, New Romney, Hythe, Dover, Sandwich and Rye. The tale that is told is that these coastal towns were required, by the English Crown, to provide and maintain ships for the use of the Crown. In return these places were given quite a number of privileges; including an exemption from certain taxes. This was around 1135 and in 1155 there was a Royal Charter.

However, there are those who believe that Cinque Ports were established earlier by "Edward the Confessor", almost a century before, when he needed to bring a group of "troublesome ports" to order, his reason was that the people of these places controlled cross-channel traffic. So I wonder if that is a part of this "freeport" idea from the Johnson mob – toss the troublesome Scots a "kind-of" Cinque Port and then if they are making money they will stay in the Union.

There was a lot of talk in the SNP about these, and the Greens were vocal in objecting. Nicola Sturgeon's government objected to the idea but the UK Government said they would be happening anyway. The establishment of "freeports" in Scotland, without the involvement of our government, would override areas of devolved competence. So the Scottish Government engaged and said well they will have to help us deliver the "green economy", to help fight climate change.

Of course there are a number of voices from Scottish business people, and some local authorities, who feel that a "freeport" in their back yard is just what they need.

PB

Maybe with that last sentence I have found it. "What THEY need" ... it may well be what THEY need to make them more money. It maybe that they make more job opportunities. However, that is not the path I want for Scotland, I want a path that says "This is what this good for the whole of Scotland", because we are Scots, this is our country and we want to make it better for everyone, not just those in the 45 miles around Rosyth, or Stranraer, Aberdeen, or wherever they end up. Oh yes you can say well the money will filter through to all parts of the country. I think that is naive economics in the UK is totally skewed towards providing shareholders with dividends and the Tory government shows very little empathy for those in society who find it very difficult to ride the various "hamster wheels" that society provides by way of employment.

Just one more idea to throw out. "The creation of jobs" is one of the selling points of these "freeports". How many news stories have you come across recently which say that there are to few people to drive HGVs, pick crops, to be bouncers outside night clubs, to be workers in care-homes, to be doctors, to be nurses. There are not enough people to do all the things that need doing now!

I do not support these, I do not think the SNP government supports these, we know that the Greens don't support these, but the UK Government will do them anyway, and trample over us yet again. Are you Yes yet?

PB

Cher Bonfis

It's time to rid ourselves of the failing graduates of Eton

Also published in 'The National' 20 February 2022 11

Tom Paxton, the folk singer, who was born in Chicago, came into my life when I was about 14 years old. I loved the sound of his voice, the words and ideas of his songs, the constant stare from his eyes as he sang when I saw him in concert. I will not try to kid you on that he is a friend but I have met him several times, once I was in the wings of a stage and stood next to him and I watched has he copied, note for note, on his guitar, the guitar playing of the fellow who was on stage performing, the guy on the stage was very good. There is a live album of Tom's, In The Orchard, from 1984.

On it is a great song, *The Bomb The Bomb We Finally Built The Perfect Bomb It Turns The Tanks To butter And The People Walk Away*. In one of the introductions on that record Tom says of the American government that he just finished writing pile of songs about a pile of mess they had made and just cleared his desk, only to discovered that a heap of new stories had just arrived; so he had to pick up his pen and write some more. Tom is 84 now, and as far as I know, he is still wrestling with the issues of the day, I suspect he might have a backlog in the wake of the Trump presidency.

It is how I feel about the world of politics here at home in Scotland there is always another awful story that needs to be addressed. Most of them emanating from the land south of our Border because of the grip of a Union that was forged from the bribery perforated, on behalf of Queen Anne and the English Parliament, by John Dalrymple, First Earl of Stair, (Stair is to the east of the town of Ayr. Dalrymple was the man who gave the orders for the Campbell militia to murder thirty eight members of MacDonald clan, in the notorious Massacre of Glencoe, in January 1692).

Lord Banff "sold" his vote for 11 pounds and 2 shillings. The Earl of Finlater sold his for 100 pounds. The Provost of Wig Town sold his for 25 pounds. Others bargained for a higher price, The Lord High Commissioner, Duke of Queensberry, James Douglas was paid 1325 pounds 10 shillings.

So by 110 votes to 68, in January 1707 Scotland's Parliament was voted out existence and article one of the Treaty of Union states that the two Kingdoms of England and Scotland are united under the name of Great Britain. Today we suffer under the yoke of the words stored on a sheet of vellum deep in the cellars of Westminster (or wherever they hide these things these days).

There were some "jolly photees" of Liz Truss, from the 10 Downing Street photographer, trying to make her look like a model, a suggestion of glamour! Trussed up in what looked almost like a bearskin at changing of the guard at Buckingham Palace. There she stood with some Russian military guys with their huge rimmed hats. I wonder if she had chartered another plane at £500000 or maybe she hitched a ride on an Aeroflot.

Last week Boris was off on a short jolly too, over to Ukraine, well after the debacle of his trip to Moscow when he was foreign secretary, I guess they would not give him a visa go to back to Russia anytime soon. Sergei Lavrov commented after that Truss had not prepared for the meeting and would not listen (a lesson learned from Theresa May?). Indeed even before she got to Moscow it is reported that she had signed papers ordering tougher sanctions on Russia, as if they care tuppence. I know that "tuppence" is from the old days, these days it is 2 pence, but the Tories want to reintroduce "imperial measurements"., and now Jacob Rees-Mogg has the job of trying to work out what the benefits of Brexit are I feel it in my water that 20 shillings in a pound might make a come back.

In the meantime, back here on earth in Scotland our government is investing record amounts in renewable energy. The highest per person investment in education in the UK – £1319 in England, £1382 in Wales but here £1685. Yet next week, or the week after, at First Minister's Questions Sarwar or Ross will get up and bleat on about "the attainment gap".

It is well known that poverty is the driving force behind this. It seems to me that in the current political arrangement, where our countries finances are ultimately controlled by the government of another country, there will always be this so called gap. What we need to be able to do is ensure that all our population can have a good standard of living and move away from the desperation where loosing £20 a week from Universal Credit plunges folk into food banks and where Brexit caused inflation gives folk sleepless nights.

Years ago I had cause to visit schools in the Highlands, some were in buildings left over from the Second World War and on more than one occasion saucepans littered the floor collecting the dips of rain water through the ceiling. Our government has built or upgraded more than 1000 schools in the past few years. There is £2 billion of investment into the learning estate in the pipeline.

Here is a dream that we, Scotland, become an independent country. We rid ourselves of the Eton-schooled leaders of Westminster, where a Tory government is so packed with talent that the choice of Foreign Secretary is really only a model for a cut-down bearskin hat. Then through our world-class education system we nurture a scientist who makes the perfect bomb which turns the tanks to butter so the people can walk away.

Cher Bonfis
I Want to Stop Writing About the Union
Social Media Post 2021

Independence for Scotland is going to be so cool. Once we are Independent I will be able to stop writing of the horror of our country being attached to England and the control over us of the government in Westminster. It is all a matter of respect.

As if it was not enough that today our First Minister is unable to roll out our own Covid ease of restrictions, because without a central bank and our own finances we have not got the power to say free testing continues. Instead our government has to rummage around in the cupboard and see if there is a little bit more money because if the English government will not provide free testing in their country any longer so there are no residual for us.

Then we learn that Boris Johnson, in answering a Metropolitan Police questionnaire into alleged Downing Street Parties, has become the first Prime Minister to answer questions 'Under Caution'.

The Pope has added his voice to the great cry from around the world, through the United Nations, that it is time for the UK government to hand back the Chagos Island Diego Garcia. Disrespect of International Law, not the first time recently.

The European Union Commission has referred the UK to the European Court of Justice; on the back of a UK Supreme Court ruling ordering the Romanian Government to pay compensation to investors who lost out on state subsidies. As if the EU were not already very tired of the UK's disrespect over Brexit and the implementation of the Northern Ireland Protocol.

The UK Electoral Commission is very concerned about some new legislation which will enable future governments to influence their operational functions and decision making.

It would be easy to fill several pages with more examples of the 'wild west' behaviour of the 'Lords and Masters' of Westminster. However it is not just them; it is all those who keep them in power, the people who vote for them and the institutions which support them. I find it strange that there are not demonstrations demanding change. You remember when Nick Clegg's lot agreed to University Fees in England. It was not so long ago, people got really upset with him whilst his Lib Dems were in cahoots with the Tories. Maybe the new laws in the 'Police, Crime, Sentencing and Courts Bill 2021' and it's 'Public Nuisance' offence is keeping them at home.

Are the English electorate happy with Boris Johnson and the things he and his Ministers are doing? Or are they forever blinded by the lights of whatever scandal is on the table today? Not to mention Putin stoking the furnace of a war that nobody in the world needs, except the arms dealers and manufacturers. This is a matter of respect and disrespect from every angle.

So is it any leap at all to think about the environment and the disrespect people have when they dump their rubbish on a street or in the countryside? To me it all comes from the idea of respect. You respect yourself, others, and all that is around you. Yet there is a Prime Minister in power who had no respect for the law his government made. Although it is not everyone, there must be many who think that these things do not matter. My daughter called and thanked me for teaching her table manners. She said that at the time she thought I was just 'going on' but she had come to understand manners are a way of respecting yourself and others.

I wonder if you could imagine the disrespect that some people in Sri Lanka must have felt over the past few years as 263 containers of recycling waste have been delivered to their shore, labelled 'used mattresses, carpets and rugs' the contents were actually rags, bandages, and human body parts. This in contravention of the Basel Convention of the shipment of hazardous material. The Sri Lanka government are looking for compensation from the UK government of several millions of pounds. Of course it was not the government who committed this crime but disrespect filters down from the top and many feel that if those at the top can get away with it why shouldn't I?

Any Scot longing for Independence will have felt the disrespect, which is the constant background noise of all Scotland's dealings with Westminster. Manners and respect are the oil and grease that lubricate the engines of our lives. It is so sad to live in a time when the UK government seems to have little respect for anything and even sadder that there is not enough self-respect within the Labour opposition party, in Westminster, to offer the good people of England an attractive and credible alternative to the sleaze of the current administration.

Patrick Harvie.

With the powers of an independent country in Europe, Scotland could do far more to decarbonise our economy and build a fairer and better economy.

PB

Cher Bonfis
Do we need a Jack Reacher or Ethan Hunt to put a stop to Vladimir Putin?
Also published in 'The National' 20 February 2022 12

I am not an avid Tom Cruise fan but whenever one of his films does cross my path I have to admire the sheer talent of the man. He is a fine actor. I am sure many people will have seen him in one of those 'Mission Impossible' films where he is dangling from a wire among laser beams which will surly trip the alarm if any part of his body crosses one or something of that ilk. One of his films from 2008 is Valkyrie. The film deals with a plot to assassinate Adolf Hitler on 20 July 1944. Cruise played the part of Claus von Stauffenberg one of central organisers of the plot. The plot ultimately failed. Although there is some argument about the exact date on which The Second World War began (Chamberlain declared war 03 September, but war had been going on between Japan and China for two years by then.) from 01 September 1939 to 20 July 1944 there were 1785 days of war from the invasion of Poland by Hitler's forces. The estimate is that around 85 million people died during World War II - that was 3% of the total population of the world about 2.3 billion people then. 83 years later the pain of this conflict is still painful to many.

I think many would argue that without Adolf Hitler there would not have been World War II. Of course there may have been another person, who had a similar vision and charisma but these things are rare in our world. Tom Cruise has a rare talent, you may well think you could do his job but there is actually only one Tom Cruise. You can line up all the great actors of the age and each is different. It is the same with dictators. Saddam Hussein, Muammer Gaddafi, Xi Jinping and the currently in the lime light, Vladimir Putin, are all very different people; but Putin is the first for 83 years to be reckless enough to engage in a conflict which, seriously, could begin a world wide war which nobody but the arms dealers and manufacturers need.

I think that the look on Sergei Naryshkin's face, he is Putin's Director of Foreign Intelligence, is anything to go by when Putin embarrassed him on live television on 22 February 2022, telling Naryshkin to 'speak plainly'. Putin has surrounded himself with people who are afraid to do anything but his bidding. Putin is not the Greek, mythological Lernean Hydra, there are not another 2 Putin's waiting in the wings to step up and fill his shoes. Putin would be to scared to allow such a situation. He has imprisoned Alexei Navalny, his political opposition. His 'Brown Shirts', in their grey uniforms, hustled the brave protesters, against the invasion of Ukraine, from Moscow streets, into vans and whisked them away to heaven knows where and who knows if they will ever be seen again?

Nicola Sturgeon got it absolutely right in her speech in out Holyrood Parliament, 24 February….. "Putin is an autocrat. His control of the apparatus of state, of the economy, the military and the media can make his power seem impregnable but as with most strong-men leaders, underneath the veneer of power lies insecurity and fear. Fear of democracy, freedom, the kind of popular uprising witnessed over recent years in Ukraine ever happening in Russia. Let us not say he is acting in the name of the Russian people..."

Putin has not the charisma of Hitler and is vision is smaller, he wants to go back to a time which has gone. There are many, it can be argued, in the Westminster Tory party who also wish to go back to the Empire and Imperial Measurements. Terrifyingly, however, both Hitler and Putin have a commonality in that their actions contain/ed the seeds which did/could bring war to the whole of Europe, once more and worse still that could spread across the globe. In the light of the superior conventional forces of the NATO powers that could lead an insecure Putin into a 'Doctor Strangelove' and a pressing of the nuclear trigger.

We are in serious need of a Jack Reacher or Ethan Hunt, a Mission Impossible, 1785 days are too many days in which the lives of many young soldiers could be lost. Where are the 'Navy Seals' and the 'SAS'? "Your mission Jim, should you decide to accept it will be to capture, alive, Valdimir Putin, President of the Russian Federation and bring him to the court in Den Haag before he commits any more crimes against humanity." You can argue that someone else would have led the world into World War Two if Hitler had not, I do not happen to think so. Putin the Hydra will not grow two more heads. If he were removed there would be a place for cooler heads and diplomacy, then democracy might stand a chance of returning to Russia.

Democracy is a fragile thing it so easily and so often slips into dictatorship. Peace is a fragile thing and we take it for granted at our peril. I was at a wedding in Switzerland and the grandfather made a speech he said "What people need is peace and stability."

Angus Robertson

"You don't have such a successful showing unless the people want the SNP to continue in government and want to see Nicola Sturgeon remain as first minister.

UK Government's response to war in Ukraine has been a total embarrassment

Also published in 'The National' 04 March 2022 13

B ack in primary school days when the warm came to the ears and you knew your cheeks were flush, 'Embarrassment rules OK'. I never liked that feeling and I always felt sorry for anyone that it happened to. How embarrassed can you be made to feel by your own government? No not our Scottish Government, I mean the bit of government we never voted for; that controls our finances, our foreign policy and our defence.

What a (not a word to be used lightly) 'stunning' performance by Daria Kaleniuk, executive director of the Anti-Corruption Action Centre of Ukraine. What perfection to see 'corruption' in that title. What a perfect candidate for her organisation to scon (flatten); the Prime Minster of the UK, Boris Johnson. You could just see the red filling his cheeks as he stood on the 'naughty step', nodding his head, in the gesture which invites the speaker to continue. "Britain guaranteed our security under Budapest Memorandum," Daria blurted. Britain did. They asked Ukraine to give up their nuclear weapons in 1994 in exchange for 'Security Guarantees'. 28 years later Ukraine blows the dust of the 'guarantee' to find there are arguments about interpretation and translations, even though they got rid of their nuclear deterrent, as agreed! I am sure some are realising that doing business with 'Arthur Daily' may mean you get a car, but it does not necessarily mean you get an engine under the bonnet to make it move.

PB

Maybe that is the exact description of the UK. these days. 'The Arthur Daily of Europe', a nice enough fellow on the face of it but the merchandise may not deliver the results you expect and may, indeed, embarrass everyone.

What if the boot was on the other foot and the UK was suffering an invasion of Valdimir Putin. What if it were British women and children, separated from their husbands and sons, fleeing across the sea to France, Belguim, The Netherlands and the Republic of Ireland. I wonder if, even after all the terrible actions in the past few years of the current Tory cabal, would they be refused entry? Would only refugees with family connections be allowed? Look at the number of refugees from Ukraine that Poland, Slovakia, and Moldova have welcomed in already. How embarrassing can it be when Priti Patel says ok if you come and pick some fruit you can stay a little while. 'Of course', she said, 'we must control because Russian troops might infiltrate groups of refugees'. Really? Ms. Patel do you really think, under current circumstances it is really necessary to make desperate people jump through hoops to find safety? Do you really think that these folk would wish to stay a moment longer in the UK than they have too?

The war is still on in Syria, nearly 7 million people have left Syria. More than 3 and a half million are in Turkey, wee Jordan welcomed over 666000. The 'brave' 'dis-United Kingdom' squeezed in just 11422. So lets give a pat on the back of 'Team Johnson' as 100000 is a good step up. There must be some room on the Britannia because, it was reported, sometime ago, about 1 million EU citizens left the UK because of Brexit.

Sanctions will not stop Putin. This is a serious message and we have to grasp it. Better than the messages on climate change. Climate change is on us and we have missed our chance to change. Will we grasp this Putin situation? I hope so but if the climate situation is anything to go by, probably not. 'Out of sight, out of mind'. The human predicament of waking up when it is all to late. It will not matter to Johnson's government, for they have bought such a lot of shame on themselves since they took control, it seems nothing can embarrass them at all. The shame and embarrassment is not only on them but the people who vote for them and support them. The Westminster Tory party MP's who could not find it in themselves to write enough letters to Graham Brady and force a vote of no confidence in Johnson.

It is a total embarrassment for Scots to listen to Johnson saying that the Ukrainians have a right to choose how they govern themselves, whilst at the same time dismissing the idea that Scots should have the right to choose how we govern ourselves.

How embarrassed will I feel when next I drive to see friends across Europe, post Pandemic and if peace allows, when alongside my Saltire, Ecosse, Scot and EU flag I will have to deface the back-end of my car with the letters UK?

I really hope we will not have to witness the embarrassment of 'Team Johnson' if Putin orders his forces to continue on into the rest of Europe once/if Ukraine is subsumed into the Russian Federation.

Alyn Smith

I am asking you to leave a light on
so we can find our way home."
speaking in the European Parliament
as Scotland was removed
from the European Union by Brexit

Cher Bonfis
Off to See the Wizard
Social Media Post 2022

Dorothy Gale and Toto followed the Yellow Brick Road. Along the way they found a Scarecrow, who wanted to find a brain. They met a Tin Woodman, who was looking for a heart and a lion who had lost his courage. They headed for the Emerald City and they found the great and mighty Wizard of Oz and then Toto pulls back the curtain and exposes the Wizard as the con man he is.

You must have watched a TV show where alone gunman holds a group of people hostage with one handgun. Everyone knows how difficult it is to shoot and how difficult it is to hit something. Yet no one challenges or jumps the guy, even though the chances of him being a marksman are slim. All they need to do is distract and knock the gun from his hand. Yet he holds all hostage.

We have seen the James Bond's taking on the megalomaniac, one man who wants to rule the world. Now we are in the situation where we really have such a 'Blofeld' and we are scared. There is no doubt that we should be.

Napoleon is said to have said 'Imagination rules the world'. Indeed Jules Verne went to the moon in 1865; Neil Armstrong got there in 1969. Before you can do anything your brain has to imagine whatever it is that has to be done.

Your body can do nothing before your brain tells it what to do.

Einstein said 'Imagination is far greater than knowledge. Knowledge is what we now know and understand but imagination is all that will be.'

Einstein also said 'The world is an evil place, not just because of those who do evil but because of those who stand by and watch'.

We need to imagine.

The Russian's are just doing what has been done before and in the panic, the Ukrainian's are responding in the best way that they can.

I am physically unable to get to Russia, my age is much older than it was, so I cannot go and fight but when I see the crowds of unarmed Ukrainian's waving their flags and shouting at Russian Tanks I cannot imagine the bravery in such action. Yet it is something extraordinarily different from reactions in other war situations. Ukrainians imagining what they can do when there is so little that they can do.

There are so many brilliant minds and people who have much greater brains than I. However I do have some gifts to bring to the table. I have lived long, I have read many books and travelled far. I also have a gift of being able write in a reasonably coherent fashion.

What I am hoping is that someone in a position to make things happen, will see this and understand that problems cannot be solved at the same level of thinking that created the problem, that was Einstein again.

You know if he were still with us he would have gone past the splitting of the atom, nuclear war and we would have some other bigger and more powerful weapon. Even if it were still in our imaginations.

Surely in Area 51 there is some imagination, a bigger more powerful thing, remembering that love is more powerful than hate, that would make Putin understand his nuclear weapons would never win against.

All the sanctions in the world will not stop this war, we need to expand our imagination and up-grade our thinking. We need to do this today.

Please if you are someone with influence read what I have written carefully. Often comments left are a couple of ill thought words. This text is serious and if you can take this seriously you may be able to bring this ridiculous situation to a close.

What Price?
Social Media Post 2022

Kathryn Samson said, on STV News, I just heard her, that Boris Johnson said he has to speak to the Saudi's about increasing oil production. I have warmed to Kathryn since she waved a £20 note under Johnson's nose and we watched as the expression on his face told us he was not really sure that a £20 note was a large enough denomination to be legal tender. The Royal Television Society pronounced Kathyrn 'Nations and Regions Presenter of the Year Award Winner'. STV should be proud. She's a feisty lass oor Kathryn.

What struck me about this story was that Boris was claiming that we have to wean ourselves off our dependency on 'Russian hydrocarbons'. Personally I have never been addicted to these, although I drive a diesel car, I really have no idea from which land the liquid I pour into the tank comes.

Patrick Harvey would say we need to wean ourselves off hydrocarbons from wherever they come. I would agree with him. I think he would go further and say we should just stop using them right now.

I have heard people speak of Johnson in glowing tones 'He is so intelligent, he speaks many languages you know. So well educated he knows his history you know.' Yes those were the words I heard!

So Boris is going off to chat with the, alleged, murderer of Jamal Ahmad Khashoggi. The 'conductor' of the Yemeni Civil War, (that has been going on since 2014, before the Prince took control in 2017), Mohammed Bin Salman. Boris is going to ask him to turn the tap on the oil gusher and allow more of the stuff up and out of the desert, to be a substitute for the oil that Russia can no longer supply. My local garage was selling diesel at £1.89 a litre today. So in away one could applaud the PM's effort. However the middle eastern oil producers have been in control of the oil supply and therefore it's price for most of my seven decades. They have probably been feeling the pinch latterly because their grip of the oil wealth has slipped what with the Americans shale and us Scots renewables, all of Patrick Harvey's pal's and me, wanting to save the planet from the catastrophe of climate change.

So now Boris jumps aboard a flight and makes the Crown Prince feel as if he is centre of attention and the prince is happy to be, once again, in the position to bargain. Really the prince could have opened the gushers many days ago, without prompting, thus exhibiting his support for Ukraine and his displeasure with Putin and his benevolence towards the ordinary folk of the world. That would have been the decent thing. Decency! Do they still print that in new dictionaries? What care has the world over the continuing fight in the Yemen? Remember Afghanistan? Just a reminder the Russian Forces did not get their way in Afghanistan, I hope those fighting in Ukraine have that message in their minds.

PB

The world seems to become less decent with each day. All the alleged crimes and misdemeanours of Boris Johnson have been blown away by this terrible war in Ukraine. Party-Gate forgotten. Wall-Paper-Wars, forgotten. Jennifer Arcuri-Affair forgotten. Did you notice he just accepted a pay rise of £2000 (there is no mechanism to reject such bounty!) where is the decency in that?

In the meantime here, we Scots, must push forward and claim our independence. India, despite World War II, gained their independence in 1947 just two years after that war ended. If, for nothing else but decency, we must grasp Independence, else we be stranded upon this island until the end of time.

We cannot continue to be tied to the constant stream of inept Tory government Secretaries of State and Ministers. Pretti Pattel in charge of our immigration, Liz Truss of our foreign affaires and all their of male and female colleagues.

Oh what a joy it would be to see Kathryn have another crack at Johnson on his return from the middle-east. 'What will be the price of a Ukrainian 'Molotov Cocktail' now Prime Minister? Did the prince, as has been reported, really make you kiss his feet?'

Nonsense
Social Media Post 2022

The mechanic told me that he needed another piece of equipment from his workshop, he told me to follow him and get myself out of the cold. The foyer of his premises was a bit dismal, grubby-mawkit. He asked me if I minded dogs and at that moment two huge Rottweilers appeared, one of them seem to take a dislike to me. They were the other side of a low gate which I did not think offered much protection. The mechanic pointed to a seat and told me I could sit, I decided not to, I think that the chair was often occupied by one or both the dogs. My car was proving to be difficult to repair and a succession of other foyer guests came and went as I waited.

After some time I was joined by a man and we picked up a conversation. He told me that he was a Tory voter. He said that nothing else made any sense. He asked "What have the SNP done for Scotland?" He did not give me an opportunity to respond. He said "Whenever the Conservatives take power they immediately sort out the benefits system so that people have enough to get by and they get everyone into work." I asked a question "When was the last time that the Tory's had been in power in the Scottish Parliament?" He said "Oh not that waste of time Holyrood. They need to close that and just do everything from London. I am speaking of London Rules."

I asked him what he thought about the scandals of 'Party-Gate' and did he think that Boris Johnson should resign over the, alleged, un-truths he has been reported to have said. The man replied "It doesn't matter. Everybody broke the Covid rules. Everyone lies. It is not important, what is important is that he gets on with his job." I said "So it matters not if the people who are our leaders tell us the truth or not?" He said "I am British not Scottish. British that is where we get our greatness from. Nothing else makes any sense."

To be provocative I said "So you don't support Independence, or even a second referendum?" He said " It makes no sense to do another referendum, a waste of money, Independence makes no sense." He repeated. He continued "Nobody likes the SNP and nobody wants another referendum." I asked "Why people have voted in such large numbers for the SNP in many elections in recent times?" He said (yes you got it) "It doesn't make sense." So I asked how the SNP enjoy so much support for their policies and for Independence. He said "Well it's the Labour party people who support Nicola Sturgeon."

Of course that made no sense to me at all but I remembered a man I met outside a polling station during Mrs. Mays election gamble. He told me that he had voted Labour because he wanted to stay in the European Union! At the time I do not think Jeremy Corbin knew which way he wanted that to go.

The sense I am trying to make here is that for all the communication available. For all the websites, television and radio, magazines and newspapers. Maybe the reintroduction of the 'Town Crier' and the 'Troubadour' might be a better way for spreading the current news. There are a lot of people who are totally confused and lost, really the Tory and Labour stars of this story are not alone in not making sense of any of the mixed up politics we are presented. I think that suits the UK Government just fine. Maybe one of their in house slogans is 'keep them confused', indeed Johnson has said 'make so many gaffs the media doesn't know which one to concentrate on.'

For you and I who want an Independent Scotland we have to lead these people to a politics that does make sense so that they can see Independence is our only sensible option for our future. With my Tory acquaintance, in the garage foyer, there really was not time to get beyond his idea of the only thing that made sense was Prime Minister Johnson continuing in office, for Holyrood to be swept away and 'London Rule' be made absolute. Still I did pose some questions and I hope that in the quiet of a night, some of the things I put forward may help him to question his loyalty to the Conservative Party. One thing is for sure I told him loudly and clearly that in my opinion the only politics that make sense is an SNP Government which takes us to an Independent Scotland.

Never forget that Brexit is the reason Britain is in such a state

Also published in 'The National' 27 March 2022 14

Thursday 23 June 2016 there were 3987112 people in Scotland who were entitled to cast a ballot. 2679513, that is 67.2% of the electorate, actually put pen to paper and bothered to cast their vote. So 62% of actual voters in Scotland thought that the people of the dis-United Kingdom would be better off as members of the European Union. Which, surprisingly, it seems to some people, must mean that 1661191 Scottish voters caught-on that outside the European Union we Scots would endure a much lower standard of living, if the UK were to relinquish membership of the European Union.

It may be that many of them listened to Pascal Lamy, former head of the World Trade Organisation, who said in the run up to the Brexit referendum that the UK exiting Europe on WTO terms was 'not hell but it was far from today's heaven'. He also likened the situation to that of a football team leaving the first division and finding itself at the bottom of the forth division.

Last September 'The Herald' newspaper reported that UK exports had decreased by 5.5% since 2016 making the UK the place amongst it's neighbours the only economy with a negative balance of trade. We have heard endless stories of the difficulties exporters face with extra red tape and huge extra costs.

The UK Government might try to say that they do not have a plan to choke off supply of labour to increase wages and decrease the number of people living on benefits. With their rhetoric over immigration and asylum seekers, their reluctance to fully engage and make it very easy for those fleeing Ukraine it suggests that that is the line they have been pursuing. Reduce supply and the price rises. At the same time they have reduced the supply of goods entering the UK and because of the increase in wages costs for businesses, prices are rising in the shops.

My question is why is this a surprise? It was not only Pascal Lamy who gave warnings.

The Johnson Government has fallen upon a stream of luck which is really unbelievable and the sad reality is that what has been lucky for them has been absolute, utter tragedy and horror for millions. The Pandemic and the now the horror of Putin's evil war on Ukraine. Have given them a smokescreen to hide their Brexit failure. Without a doubt these awful things have added problems but Brexit is the enormous economic issue.

It is my thought that Brexit was a factor in Putin's thinking when he decided, for whatever disgusting reason, to send his weapons and troops into Ukraine. He had a notion that the EU was less strong, less united, with the rumblings from Poland and Hungry and the UK's exit.

So all the hype and nonsense of Rishi Sunak and his 'Spring Statement' today lead me back to the same question as I asked above 'Why is all this a surprise?'. I am sorry I cannot warm to this Sunak man at all, a millionaire at the despatch boxes doing a very weak impression of a master trader on the Barras, Gallowgate. 'Not one, not even by two, but by five pence per litre.' The sentences before that were full of bluster about how big and strong the UK economy is and we should be happy for that because it allows 'us' to fund our defence and to send help to Ukraine. Heavens we should help Ukraine, in 1994 we promised to and if anyone in Government had had the forethought that would have snuggled a wee nest egg away for that rainy day. Then again the UK has two trillion pounds of debt.

Planning for the future that is not the way of things in the UK. The UK is always 'Oh my we didn't expect that, now what do we do?' The fortune in that is that the UK population is very good in a crisis and the good women and men step up and give all they have to pull inept Governments out of the mire they continually make.

My heart is heavy with the sadness of Ukraine and I am incensed that we are still tied to the rUK where a Chancellor can boast about the great, strong, wealth of the nation and yet do absolutely nothing to help ordinary, everyday, people who were hardly getting by before 6% inflation. Then again it is no surprise and there will be many here in Scotland who consider that strong economy of the UK as something to be voted for. As Sunak with his smoke and mirrors blinds them with his nonsense yet again. To all those people, I know they will never read this, please think, we are Scotland and we are big enough, strong enough, clever enough and rich enough to do so, so much better as an independent country.

Dame Evelyn Glennie

Scotland has never ceased to amaze the world with its forward vision, bold action, and great educational institutions. Nothing makes me more proud than to promote this wonderful land with all its richness and diversity wherever I go.

Respect
Social Media Post 2022

President Biden said at the beginning of his term that anyone showing disrespect for another would be instantly dismissed.

I saw it printed on the stern of a P&O ferry, declaiming it's port of registry. I flew back through time in my mind to a January thirty years ago, in the morning we went skiing in the Troodos Mountains and later in the day we were on the beach near Limassol, it was pleasantly warm. Nicosia was the wrenching part of that tour, the fence and unoccupied houses which formed the separation between the Turkish north and the Greek south of the island of Cyprus.

My mind is never far from the issue of independence for Scotland, I have craved it all my life. Not because of any dislike for our neighbours but for the greater respect of Scotland and our people. I have long thought that England would feel more comfortable in it's own shoes, if it could just concentrate upon itself (it mostly does that anyway). Indeed I think one of the great issues in the tragedy of Brexit was the English nation crying out to be heard in a world that has largely lost it's respect for the former empire builder.

PB

The world has lost respect because the UK has largely lost it's own self respect. It is demonstrated in the Prime Minister, I watched Boris Johnson, looking like a shabby deputy head-teacher from a run-down 1970's comprehensive school, whilst the other heads of the NATO alliance shook hands in their smart 'unshevelled' suits. There was a whiff of disrespect around Johnson 'I don't need to look smart, I am good enough as I am', was the message his lost body language was shouting. The other leaders heard it loud and clear and ignored him. Their feelings were, probably, 'we have had enough disrespect from this guy'.

Respect yourself and thus you can respect others. I remind you of this phrase from Nicola Sturgeon 'most strong-men leaders, underneath the veneer of power lies insecurity and fear.'

So why is it that populations of people around the world continually to allow men of low self-worth to become powerful leaders? Why do we allow them to silence, imprison and kill their opposition?

When President Biden said that Putin had to go, I thought 'wow at last a leader who is going to stand up and be counted. The leader of the free world is going to make a stand'. Moments later the White House staff and the Secretary of State were walking that back. Whilst the brave people of Ukraine do their best impression of the little Dutch boy who put his finger in the dwijk. Whilst the rest of the world place bets on how long it will be before a sea of Russian military burst the dam and we are all engulfed in the flood. (Foot Notes: How will Putin stand trail for war crimes if he is still President of the Russian Federation? Also a bit of praise for Johnson from President Zelensky who thanked him for the support in weaponry provided by the UK, but remember when Ukraine gave up their nuclear weapons the UK guaranteed their security in exchange.)

What do we do in a world that is swimming in disrespect? Where many leaders display minimal levels of self-respect. Where countries fail to respect each others borders? Where we Scots have still to find that little bit more courage, self-respect, that would make it totally clear to all, that we accept nothing other than the complete respect of all 195 countries that Scotland is an independent sovereign nation.

Where is the courage and the might of the American military, the NATO alliance? What is the point of the filthy nuclear war head stock pile at Faslane if all Putin has to do is to threaten to use some of his?

For my money the whole thing is about respect for self and respect for others. The Ukrainian people are exhibiting their self-respect for all they are worth.

Whilst we are engulfed in an ocean of disrespect. From the Westminster politicians who fail to understand that Scotland is a country with it's own parliament. A Prime Minister who cannot grasp the idea that Scots vote for things that they want and democratically those things should be respected. I could continue with a list that would fill more than this page. I know that many of our fellow Scots lap up all of this like a cat at a bowl of cream.

Robert Burns

For a' that, an' a' that,
It's coming yet for a' that,
That Man to Man, the world o'er,
Shall brothers be for a' that.

John Swinny

A revolution suggests you dump everything.
That would be folly....

Join the Dots
Social Media Post 2022

I used to like games when I was a wean, 'Join the Dots' and I would draw a line between 1 and 2, and 2 and 3. My faither's favourite was 'boxes', we took it in turns to draw lines between dots and so make boxes into which we would write our initials. These games were fun and they helped in my education. These games taught strategy and promoted the idea the if you join the dots, in the correct order, you might get a picture.

I have no idea if the students of Eton ever got to play those sorts of games with their nannies. I watched the Secretary of State for Business, Energy and Industrial Strategy squirming on the television yesterday, I understand he went to a state primary school and then on to an Independent Preparatory school, where he cleverly won the Harrow Prize and then he when on to Eton. As with probably all the current UK Secretaries of State and Ministers there is often a blank look on their faces when they are interviewed, giving the suggestion that joining the dots to complete the picture had never crossed their mind.

There was a clip of 'The Secretary of State for Digital, Culture, Media and Sport', being quizzed by Damian Green, Nadine Dorries obviously had no idea of how the television station, 'Channel 4', is funded, but actually one wonders how on earth

'Digital, Culture, Media and Sport' could have dots joined in such away as to make a picture.

I actually watched from the gallery in the Westminster Parliament one day as the then Secretary of Education, Michael Gove, droned on about his plans to shake everything up and make it fit for purpose. It is an interesting experience sitting in such a place, unlike watching it on television you can be your own editor and look at all the MP's as they watch the person at the despatch boxes. You can see the boredom, the hidden yawns, those looking at the screens of their phones and occasionally the ones who are really interested in what is being said. I would say you could see them trying to join the dots, trying to make a picture. After all a picture paints a thousand words.

On every occasion that I am able to engage in conversation with my fellow Scots I try to declare my interest and longing for an independent Scotland. I have many methods of bringing the subject to the fore. Sometimes I get a tart reaction and if that ever happens I ask questions and listen, my hope is always that maybe they will see the dots, understand the numbers and be able to join a straight line between two of them at least to start building a better picture in their minds.

It is strange to me that Kwasi Kwarteng was unable to join the dots between the recent event in 'oor Glasgie' called COP 26 and squeezing all the oil and gas possible from the North Sea, yet the person who did his job before him was Alok Sharma, the man who ran the COP 26 event.

Jacob Rees-Mogg said something to that effect, as Minister of State for Brexit, that he is still searching for the opportunities of Brexit, I think that they are two dots which will be very hard to find, let alone draw a line between. Rees-Mogg has a host of recent statements ... 'people have moved on from party-gate', 'Boris was given the wrong information on lockdown parties', 'Boris did not mislead parliament', 'God made Men and Women'. It is hard to even find the dots in all of that, let alone join them.

With all of that and so, so, much more, the last two Scottish people I have spoken with about independence have both stated they are for the European Union and for the United Kingdom. I suggested that maybe the United Kingdom, of which they wished they could still belong to, had disappeared a long time ago and that the dots no longer join up. Further I pointed towards some of the joined up thinking we can see within our own Scottish Government, for example, 'poverty leads to most of societies problems, so lets make childhood a priority and see if we can lift a generation out of poverty'. A baby box so all get a chance at a good start.   £20 a week child payment, 1140 hours of funded early learning and child care. Now there are some dots that add up and start to make a picture of a brighter future for oor weans. Then horror upon horror! The Chancellor of the Exchequer puts his oar in the water and splashes away much of the benefit, of all that Scottish joined up thinking.

You and I should take a sheet of paper and a pencil with us on every outing and engage people in a game of join the dots, there are still many Scots who have yet to understand how the dots joining Scotland to the rUK fail to make a proper picture and prevent us being the nation we could be, leading the way, joining the dots, as Scots have always done.

Maria Montessori

Independence is not a static condition; it is a continuous conquest, and in order to reach not only freedom, but also strength, and the perfecting on one's powers, it is necessary to follow this path of unremitting toil.

One rule for the Conservative party liars, another for the rest of us poor saps

Also published in 'The National' 17 April 2022 15

"Hey MacKenzie, I saw it on TV, we need not obey the law anymore!" "What you say Muckle-Jaw?" "I saw it on the TV; some big boss man, he sacked a load of people at P&O Ferries, he said he knew he was breaking the law but he did it anyway. Then, and here's the good bit, he said he would break the law again! "Didn't the Polis come Muckle-Jaw?" "No MacKenzie, the man was answering questions in them 'Houses of Parliament', you know that place down in England. They questioned him and nobody did a thing!" "That's unbelievable Muckle-Jaw." "There is more. That Prime Minister, the one with the untidy hair who looks like a deputy headmaster of a seventies comprehensive school, they said he and that bloke who lives next door to him, the one with the supercilious smile, went to 'lock down parties', during that Pandemic and the polis gave them a fine. Well you'd think high-ups like that would loose their jobs for that. When you think of all the lads and lassies that died!" "Oh I don't know Muckle-Jaw, there is a war on!" "MacKenzie. Did that stop Christopher Foyle? No it didn't, all the way through the Second World War he kept on catching the murderers!" "Muckle-Jaw that was just a TV show!" "I know, 'Foyles War' but this law breaking is real and if they can get away with it I suggest we can too." "What are you saying Muckle-Jaw?"

"Well you know me and the boys have been planning that big job? It's on tonight." "Muckle-Jaw don't be stupid you'll get caught." "MacKenzie then so will you! You're driving the car remember? It won't matter even if we are caught the law in England means nothing any more." "Muckle-Jaw but we live in Scotland!" MacKenzie wiped the perspiration from is brow and said "pew!"

When the Tories were baying for Nicola Sturgeon's 'blood', when she was accused of breaking the 'Ministerial Code' she called on her Deputy John Swinney and told him that if she were found to have broken it, he would have to step up to the First Minister position.

What a contrast to the behaviour of Johnson and all the Tory MP's who fail to send letters of no confidence. Twisting and swivelling as an eel stuck in a drain pipe. The claim that the 'sainted' Johnson is the only one who can sort out the situation in Ukraine is ludicrous. Sadly of the 273 men and 87 women, who make up the parliamentary Conservative Party, there is no one with ambition enough to tap Johnson on the shoulder and tell him that his turn is over, move aside.

They and the Labour Party should be circling like Great White Sharks in the James Bond Movie, 'Thunderball'. Instead the 'one-and-only' 'BJ' is making a mockery of the office he holds, and turning the rule of law into something that only applies to those outside his Government.

What next? Will there be a suspension of elections because of 'The War'?

The question that we should all be concerned with is what are the Prime Ministers personal ambitions?

Look around the world at the fragile democracies that so effortlessly fall into dictatorships.

I have survived Churchill, Eden, MacMillian, Douglas-Home, Wilson, Heath, Callaghan, Thatcher, Major, Blair, Brown, Cameron and May, however I feel about any of these none of them had such a disregard of 'The Right Thing To Do' as Johnson. Will you and I survive Johnson?

I have longed to be free of this United Kingdom since primary school days when I first started to understand how precious being Scottish is. I ask myself everyday why I have not been more successful in helping the union supporting Scots that I am acquainted with to see themselves as not as British but as Scottish. Never fear I will continue armed with all this new ammunition, I will keep chipping away and with fortune, come Indyref2, enough of us will say YES to a new Scotland that respects the rule of law and democracy. A country of people who can be a beacon for democracy in a world that has lost it's way in many lands.

I am not a 'John Knoxian', but he and George Buchanan did have it that 'power is not vested in kings, nobles or clergy but IN THE PEOPLE; who were expected to defend that political power against any interloper'.

Scotland: We really have to stand now and be counted. As if there were not enough mandates for Indyref2, we must provide another 05 May 2022.

Sean Connery

Scotland should be nothing less than equal with all the other nations of the world.

Stench of superiority still lingers for Boris Johnson and his colleagues

Also published in 'The National' 24 April 2022 16

In 1978 colleagues and I went to Germany on a work trip with our boss who was an English man. He was a good man and we got along well. I will always remember the reaction of my fellows when the coach stopped at a petrol station and we disembarked. On our return to the coach every person remarked on the cleanliness and that the toilets flushed because an electronic sensor detected when a person moved away from the facility. Not only that simply putting one's hands beneath the spigot caused warm water to cascade into the basin. There were many comments about who won the war and other such nonsense. The thing was that none of this 'British' contingent had any notion that such miracles were available until that day.

My boss led me into a beautiful German department store, an assistant approached, my boss adopted a loud and supercilious voice telling the young women that he only wanted to look. The assistant replied in good English that that was fine and to call upon her if there was anything that she could do to help. That was the first moment when I saw the 'British' idea of shouting at the 'natives', loud, in English and they will understand, or owe betide them.

From my observation I am certain that this inane, insane, idea of the 'Englishman's' superiority still lives on. 'Downton Abbey' still has many fooled as they genuflect to the master and doff their hat to the lady. Johnson seems to feel he has the right to get away with all manor of misdemeanours for he is the 'chosen one' and he seems to think he is better than the rest of us.

There is something inside many Scots, that says that they should doff their caps and accept our place in the world, stay in 'The Union', we cannot do without the Queen. So the Tory elite try out their 'Poll Tax' on us first. They dump their nuclear waste far from London under our ground. They test anthrax on one of our islands. Whisky and oil revenues evaporate into the UK treasury. They tell us to be grateful for the money 'gifted' during the Pandemic. We are so lucky, they tell us, to have all those good jobs secured by the 'ultimate deterrent', after all Putin has threatened he will use his. Our First Minister enters a barber shop, where no one is wearing a face mask, and momentarily forgets to sport hers and the Tories shout for resignation. Whilst Johnson holds lockdown parties galore and there are not 50 of his MP's who will say they lack confidence in him, 'he must be the superior one'.

As Johnson once again avoids answering a question by saying I DON'T THINK THAT IS WHAT PEOPLE ARE INTERESTED IN…..WHAT I THINK IS…… The 'what I think' so ladened with 'superiority' you can smell it.

The Tories reject 'refugees' as superiority chip clicks in and the background sound is 'we are surely better than them'. Refugees are seen as 'cost'. When a vision of them being able, skilled people, with knowledge and expertise which could be very valuable to all here. What if they are economic migrants? Could that not be a wonderful thing? People who have staked everything on coming to look for employment and a better life. What an opening to a CV 'I wanted to much to be here, I walked across Africa, and swam the Mediterranean, what do you need me to do?'

Hey! Refugees we in Scotland have been haemorrhaging people since 1750. During this year, Jan to March 2022 12087 new Scots were born but 16177 died. We are looking for good folk to become 'Scots by Choice'. We hope you will love it here and settle, if you do you might want to help us to Independence because your vote will count too. We will not shout loudly in Scots or English expecting you to understand, you will get used to our funny wee ways soon enough.

Could it be that the element of superiority which seems endemic in the current Westminster administration is maintained, at least in part, by seeing others has having less value? Surely that is part of the idea that dips down the walls of the Johnson flat in Downing Street, 'not for us that cheapo wall paper from B&Q'! All that nonsense in the Pandemic and formerly in the Cameron administration, 'We are all in this together'! Yes but I read 'Animal Farm' and George Orwell got it right with 'No animal can sleep in a bed' which later morphed into 'No animal can sleep in a bed with sheets'. Nothing but Egyptian cotton 1000 thread, superior quality, of course.

Annie Lennox

An independent Scotland, pursuing a clean, green and peaceful agenda, can be at the forefront of efforts against climate change.

These will be elections about decency – will England still back the Tories?

Also published in 'The National' 02 May 2022 17

A Tory MP watched some 'adult content' on a mobile phone whilst he sat in a seat in the House of Commons and he did so in a way as to draw the attention of female colleagues, who were greatly offended by that which they witnessed. Of course if that man had a gram of decency he would not have done what he did. I could not careless if he watches pornography in private but in his work place, a very public work place, well you have to ask yourself what kind of fool would do that? Of course if he had any decency he would have immediately resigned from his position and disappeared into retirement. You and I know that decency is not an asset easily found within the Parliamentary Conservative Party. After all, if he had a gram (sorry an ounce) of decency the leader of the Conservative Party would have tendered his resignation many weeks ago. Or fifty of his MP's would have written letters of no confidence.

If the current UK Government had any decency they would do the United Nation's bidding and return Diego Garcia to the Maldives. However there is little likely hood of that happening.

As the deluge of new law gushes from Westminster, much of

it undermining our own Scottish Parliament and going against the will of many Scottish people. We are being drowned in a flood of things which seem to me to lack decency. Selling off Channel 4 and requiring programme makers to brand British, two recent examples. It seems like another step to full control over the mass media.

The way I see this is that slowly and bit by bit the UK is moving further to the right of politics. That is something which I find an abomination. One would think that the left side of that equation would be working flat out to wrestle power and at least bring in back to nearer the centre of things. Sadly that weired thing 'charisma' is lacking in the front row of the English and Scottish Labour parties and sadly that is the one thing that Johnson has. No not it the way of a John F Kennedy but he has a 'weired charisma' that many English voters seem sucked in by. I hesitate to suggest that these voters are not decent people and fortunately votes are cast anomalously, so no one gets to know who supported the Conservatives at any given point.

On Thursday, many of the Council seats in England will be contested and although local elections they will no doubt send a clear message as to what many ordinary folk feel about the 'Dodge City of Westminster'. Will they tell Johnson that his Government and Party are going in the wrong direction or will they tow the line and bolster the support for reprehensible behaviour?

If the vote comes out in favour of Johnson what then for us in Scotland? Still shackled to the Union and still hosting many Scots who are happy to be ruled over by an English Parliament.

I shall get about as much as I can over the next days and I will start conversations with as many people as I can, I will urge them to vote for Scotland's Independence. We can do little in England but we can show that Scotland rejects what is currently on offer through the Westminster system. I know these are local elections but if you really want those bins emptied, those pot holes mended and a society where people are not reliant on food banks we have to put the power into our Parliament so that we can build a better home for all Scots.

I have had the fortune to travel widely and find it so hard to reconcile that our country, for decades a huge oil producer, now a huge supplier of green energy, has such a vast number of people who struggle to pay normal every day expenses.

By my way of thinking 05 May 2022 will be an election about decency. I still believe that the majority of Scots are decent folk. I hope they will cast their votes in a suitable manor.

My post-election appeal to the Yes family: put any differences aside

Also published in 'The National' 09 May 2022 18

L et it be heard; loud and tremendous, applause, for all our bonnie lassies and callants who took the time to vote in local elections last week. Thank you to those who sort to use their vote in the cause of our independence.

The score card has demoted Mr. Ross of Moray and his Tory Party into the third division and however the English Broadcasting Corporation try to big up Mr Sarwar it is the SNP who now have 453 council seats giving Scotland yet another mandate for IndyRef2.

Hallelujah, our bid to be rUK free just took another positive turn as Northern Ireland have voted for Michelle O'Neill and Sinn Féin, and although there is a way to go, it has taken 100 years for them to get this far, from the look on the faces of those women of Sinn Féin the border poll is closer now than before. Before anyone says that that is in the gift of Boris Johnson, he and we know that the will of the people must prevail. If you are tempted to underestimate this imagine yourself as an anti-war protester, right now, in Moscow bundled into a grey van never to be seen again. Or a fighter for democracy in Hong Kong whisked away to a correction camp in mainland China. Or a woman in Afghanistan whose rights have been totally stripped from her by over zealous interpretations of religious text. Or a Uyghur in China whose freedom to worship has been removed. Or an East German citizen before the Berlin-Wall fell with no political choice but communism.

We must count our votes and keep counting them at all elections and referenda. We need people to know and understand how important their vote is and teach children to be the voters of the future. All of us who want freedom for Scotland must, each and everyday, do all that it takes to gain our independence. Then we must do all we can to protect Scotland from ever falling into the abyss of dictatorship and one party rule. That should be written into our constitution in indelible ink. The ruling party's must be voted into office, by a majority of citizens, at regular intervals.

I talk to anyone I meet in my daily life. Whenever I can I talk of Scottish independence and I listen to what people have to say. Often I am amazed by the breadth and depth of the knowledge and engagement people have. On occasion I am saddened by the lack of awareness and the understanding, even of rudimentary concepts, that others fail to have and who seem to live in total confusion.

The Pandemic has changed the dynamics with in certain parts of our YES movement. The organisers of our great marches for independence have split into three. Alba has been created. The Johnson administration has done many things to fire up and anger many Scots who may not have been paying attention before. Whichever way you have started going my urge to you is that we do unite in one clear, loud and unassailable voice to let the rest of the world know and understand, we will be an independent nation, where the people are sovereign and we are governed by those who have been properly elected by us.

I know that there is great unrest within the ranks of Alba suggesting that the SNP are more interested in the day job than getting Indyref2 up and running. I know that there are people who say that the SNP are kidding us on about a vote next year. Well I think we are heading for a vote next year, and I am banking on it providing us with our independence.

So my appeal is that every member of our huge and wonderful YES family - put any differences aside. Leave the questions of EU membership and the monarchy until later. For now let us all commit to talking everyday about our wishes for the future of a rich, forward looking, engaged country, holding our heads high and leading, as our forbearers so often did. There is method in doing a good day job for the better the governance the more people are attracted to it. Therefore the more people there will be to vote YES next year.

UK's sums don't add up because our oil revenue has all been squandered

Also published in 'The National' 16 May 2022 19

One plus one equals two. Once times two is two. Eleven times twelve is one hundred and thirty two. Twenty-one divided by four is five point two five (actually it was five and quarter in my day). This was stuffed into my head in school. Numbers and letters, printed large and hung on the walls. We were such sweet wee weans. Since those halcyon days when Miss. Tomkins showed us arithmetic much has been distorted or completely lost. Now numbers often do not add up at all, they are banded around with imprudent abandon and come to mean little. Add the % sign and the whole façade becomes a smokescreen that can blind us from reality.

Johnson in Scandinavia signing papers guaranteeing security! The people of Ukraine got a shock when they found their 1994 deal less substantive than they had imagined when they gave up their nuclear weapons. No one questioned 'how that would be paid for, if push and shove came together?' I am for helping the Ukrainian people against the awful Russian aggression and that Sweden and Finland should have UK support. As a matter of conscience agreements must be honoured.

We know Johnson's forte, 'spending money'. Nuclear-weapons, nuclear-power stations, new royal yachts, you can make a list yourself.

What got me started on this particular rant was a BBC 'propaganda' video. A new nuclear-power station for Angelsea. 'Normal' folk proffering views, there was one voice against but the thrust was 'this is a good thing' and 'what other choices do we have?'

Saudi Arabian Aramco oil, owned by Saudi Arabia, have increased profits of 82% percent, knocking the Apple Corporation off the top of the wealth pile, since Russia invaded.

At the beginning of this screed I demonstrated the vastness of my memory, my grip on the reality of arithmetic, so that despite my ancientness, my brain still has agility. I clearly remember the bitter feelings of 19 September 2014 when our independence was pushed into the future. The sleekit nonsense around the vanishing pool of oil. 7 years on and despite COP 26 Glasgow, the UK Government use the vicious attack by Putin to open up the pipes again and even to explore a bit more. Kwasi Kwartang wants to 're-classify' natural gas as 'green-energy' to entice more investment.

In the meantime, the largest sovereign wealth fund, amassed by the Norwegians from their years of exploiting the fossil fuels of the North Sea, have allocated 10 billion Norwegian

Krone into renewable energy projects. I have been to Norway. I have been in middle eastern countries. I have been to the land of Hassanal Bolkiah, the Yang-Di Pertuan of Brunei, he has amassed a fortune of $25 billion from oil. From what I was able to see in these places 'ordinary people' seemed to live in reasonable comfort.

The Saudi's are richer and richer pumping oil. Johnson went down there, we are told, to ask them to pump a bit more, or was it the opposite? For the basic economics say the fewer barrels supplied the higher the price. Higher prices lead oil producing countries to more wealth. The world produces over 77000000 barrels of oil each day (2017 figures). In the past few years Russia produced almost one eighth of that. Wheat prices are another concern. In 2019 the total production was nearly 767 metric tons. Of which Ukraine produced nearly 29 metric tons.

The sums do not add up. The UK Government could be rubbing it's hands together with so much oil money pouring in, one could wonder why they are not taking on more civil servants to distribute the cash, instead of shedding 91000 to save money. Why does the increase in oil revenues not balance out the cost of living for us every day Scots? A simple answer is that all the oil money, from the 1970's until today, has been mismanaged, Miss. Tomkins must be looking down from her cloud wondering why Scotland is not Independent and what in heaven, or on earth, she taught me when she said one plus one equals two.

Mhairi Black

There is one thing I have to give Westminster
credit for before I go. The UK is in the
Guinness Book of World Records
As the country from which most countries have
gained independence. Since 1939 62 countries
have gained independence....and not a single one
has ever looked back.....Only one country has
decided stay and look where it has got us....
Let us be 63

Miss. Tomkins
Social Media Post 2022

Miss. Tomkins suddenly filled the screen of my latest dream. Sixty and more years since the last time I saw her and she looked not one day older than when we sweet wee weans sat up straight in our classroom and she regaled us with her knowledge and wisdom. It was just a wee primary school, in the back of nowhere in particular, well that is what the posh toffs down in London would have thought, I am sure, to us we lived in paradise. No we were not swimming in oceans of money but we were fed and for the most part we were loved, even when we were naughty. If you have read other things by me you may have come across Miss. Tomkns before. Now I am a pensioner she is still with me, in the same way that my driving instructor Mr. Jones is omnipresent each time I drive my car. These great people are still very much alive in my head even though they surely passed many years ago. It was Miss. Tomkins who taught me so much, not just to add up and take away but to sort and a think about things in my own way.

I read today how Rishi Sunak and his wife Akshata Murty had 'made it' to the Sunday Times 'Rich List'. Miss. Tomkins tapped me on the shoulder and asked me what kind of accolade I thought that was? Then she explained the word 'accolade'. She told me about the Knights from the middle ages who were 'dubbed' by having a sword rested on each shoulder. I though about people being rich and people being poor. I knew that when I was a wean all of us were 'poor'. However poor is a relative subject, can we be poor without someone else being rich?

It is said that Elon Musk has a fortune of $268 billion. Jeff Bezos has $150 billion. Benard Arnault has $132 billion and Bill Gates has $127 billion. I could continue the list but Miss. Tomkins would have asked if I had understood by now so you can extrapolate on your own.

Back to Sunak and his wife and should we give her a round of applause for giving up that 'Non-Dom' thing? I think no as even paying the extra tax will change nothing in their household. Well I could be wrong but I read that in dividends on shares from 'Infosys' she received a little short of £12 million last year. Besides Akshata's husband brings home £81932 for being an MP and then he gets £71090 for being Chancellor of the Exchequer, not to mention other sources of income, how appropriate that he represents RICHmond in North Yorkshire. Although I wonder just how rich the majority of his constituents are. I heard that the 'average wage' of a UK 'Citizen', (Or are we all 'Subjects of her Majesty' having left the EU. Always remember:- we Scots are 'Citizens' and Sovereignty resides in us.) is £29600. Even that sounds a huge amount to me.

I suppose I had better just say that this is not a 'sour-grapes' message. I get by on my pension, I really am far to busy to have to worry about what on earth to do with the kind of money Elon Musk has, my brain is limited in such capacity. There is a strange thing 'they say' Elon has $268 billion stashed away but when he said he would buy 'Twitter' he needed the backing of some of the worlds wealthiest investors', and he needed 'loans' secured on the value of 'Tesla' and 'Twitter'. One might think that if you had a fortune of $268 billion it would be easy enough to write a cheque for $44 billion and not worry about paying for heating or eating.

I listened to a Union leader demanding a pay increase for train drivers, I do not begrudge train drivers a good salary but it did strike me that some, apparently, get £54k per year. Which is a good deal more than 'average wages' and a good deal more than my pension. Then I heard Sunak say he could not help everyone "I wish I could solve every problem and, sadly, I can't and have tried to be honest about that." Miss Tomkins would have asked me why he had the job then? You could see she was fizzin. Even at such a young age Miss. Tomkins set my mind afire with questions. She told us there were about 3 to 4 billion people in the world, back then. Today there are almost 8 billion. The UK has coming up for 68 million. Here in Scotland we have about 5.5 million people.

So here is the question Miss. Tomkins would have put to us if she was with us today.....If Mr. Sunak and his wife were to 'level-up' 5.5 million Scottish people, baring in mind that there are some Scots who already have enough money, how much money would Mr. Sunak and his wife have to give from their own private funds so that everyone in Scotland received the average wage of £29600 in 2022?

Kelvin MacKenzie

Scottish independence would mean...
"Finally the Jocks will be off the payroll"

François-Marie Arouet
Voltaire

Injustice in the end produces independence

Iain Duncan Smith wants to see all us keep working until we're 75

Also published in 'The National' 25 May 2022 20

How many times I have been appalled by the policies bought forward by Iain Duncan Smith? It is difficult to count. He was born in Auld Reekie and served in the Scots Guards but it would be difficult to say that he was not a 'typical', middle/upper class, Tory from one of the home counties of England. He rose to the 'dizzy' heights of Tory Party Leader. He was the Member of Parliament for Chingford and Woodford Green until 1997.

Some of the things that he an I disagreed upon would be:- The European Union, he is 'Eurosceptic', as they would say back in the days of John Major. Universal Credit and making it more difficult for sick and disabled people to claim benefits. Sending debt collectors to reclaim 'overpaid' benefits. He published 'fake' testimonies from people who said that they 'enjoyed' having their benefits cut. The two-child policy, better known as the 'rape –clause'. Then this one that I found back in about 2001-2 to be unbearable, his views on the adoption of children to gay and unmarried people and that adoption should be kept within racial types. That last bit made me so angry, I recall shouting back at my radio and I wrote to him.

Prime Minister—'mess up the Brexit Referendum and then leave everyone else to sort out the mess Cameron', gave Duncan Smith the job of 'Secretary of State for Work and Pensions' in 2010. One the first things Duncan Smith did was to make it illegal for companies to force people to give up work at the age of 65. Then he brought in rises to the state pension age, that were provided by the Pensions Act 1995 and then his department produced the Pensions Act 2011, which accelerated the timetable of raising pension ages, so that women would get their state pension from April 2016 at the age of 63, and then from November 2018 from the age of 65. Duncan Smith wanted to go further and raise the pension age for women to 66 by October 2020 by which time the retirement age for men would have reached 66 years of age also. So many women joined the organisation 'Women Against State Pension Inequality', WASPI. They claimed that the Government failed to give them proper notification of the changes to the law. On 15 September 2020 the Judges from the Court of Appeal decided that women had not been discriminated against. Many WASPI women continue their fight for justice although many have sadly past away whilst their retirement plans were ruined.

Over in France many people have been very angry about the retirement age going up from 60 to 62 years and then, more recently, the push to 64, and more recently still Macron, in the Presidential Campaign, proposed raising the retirement age to 65.

In Netherlands retirees get 101% of their wages as a pension, in Turkey they get 102% and Croatia people get 129% of their wages! By stark contrast pensioners in the UK, according to the World Economic Forum web site, receive the worst pension deal in the developed world. (Even taking into account that in the UK the NHS should care for us from the 'cradle to the grave' so 'free!' health-care), UK pensions are just 29% of wages. EU countries on average pay 71%, in the USA it is 49% and wait for this in people in China get 83%!

In my daily trawl through the news this morning, Iain Duncan Smith's face appeared alongside a caption saying that he thought the UK retirement age should be 75 years. I remembered that figure from his 'Centre for Social Justice' two or three years ago. I could not find the article later but did see that on Saturday Duncan Smith did make an appeal for benefits to be raised in line with inflation, immediately. That may have been how the 75 years cropped up again. I thought if that's what Iain says things really must be much, much, much, much worse that I thought.

I cannot say that I had ever thought of retiring, but sadly bits of my body are crumbling and frankly I feel lucky that the bit between my ears still has some functionality, I have not yet got to 75 but sadly there are many things beyond may capabilities now. How are you doing you over 66's?

If you are a UK pensioner, here in Scotland, hanging onto

your expenditure as best you can, without the 'triple lock', that Sunak stole away a short time ago, remember that at the SNP conference, I think it was 2019, in Auld Reekie, it was made policy that in an Independent Scotland pensions should be bought into line with those in Europe, the figure I heard quoted then was about £355.00 per week. Food for thought as the debate for Indyref2 has begun.

Henry Ford

If money is your hope for independence
you will never have it

Be engaged, interested
and let's rid ourselves of the Tories forever

Also published in 'The National' 29 May 2022 21

I think I have worked it out! Of all jobs in the world an MP at Westminster, for all the downside that incumbents may claim is a pretty good number. Nice money, lots of perks, nice pension. Right now not all but many Tory MP's have throbbing heads full of blurred photographs, their leader toasting yet another lockdown party in number ten. Photos taken whilst continuants were dying of Covid. These Tories know if a General Election happened tomorrow, they would loose their seat. No wonder Graham Brady's letter box is not stuffed full of letters expressing no confidence in Boris Johnson. It is all about the individual doing well, what about the rest of the people? *'Really? That's nothing to do with me. Inflation. Why do you winge and whine so?'*

Speaking of letters, the editors who deal to letters to 'The National' have kindly printed many of my missives, not all of them, for example 16 February 2022, a week before Putin's forces began to kill Ukrainian people, I wrote a piece called 'Engage be Interested'. The title came from a speech I heard Ailie Ross-Oliver make outside our Parliament on the dreadful night that Scotland was torn out of the European Union. Ailie's speech was powerful, she spoke of young Scots and she said 'we are engaged, we are interested'. The rest of my article was a global tour of dictators and the first was Putin. The question I posed: Does Boris Johnson have dictatorship dreams?

I love listening to Mhairi Black and understood exactly what she said when she said that the UK is sleep walking ever closer to fascism. I refer you to paragraph one above, where the people in Government may seem to care more for their own salary than they care for their constituents and their country.

Scotland has longest serving First Minister, respected around the world. We have more mandates for Indyref2 than a hedgehog has spines. Our Parliament is working all the time currently on these subjects. Coronavirus (Recovery and Reform), Disabled Children and Young People (Transitions to Adulthood), European Charter of Local Self-Government (Incorporation), Fireworks and Pyrotechnic Articles, Gender Recognition Reform, Good Food Nation, Hunting with Dogs, Non-Domestic Rates (Coronavirus), Scottish Local Government Elections (Candidacy Rights of Foreign Nationals) Bill, United Nations Convention on the Rights of the Child (Incorporation).

In the meantime, down in Westminster, the Prime Minister is so 'humbled' and has 'learned such a lesson' from Sue Gray's 'Part-Gate' report, that the only action he will take is to 'STAY IN OFFICE'. After all 'Murray Ross' says "there is a war on!" It is not only Johnson who has no shame, his so-called deputy Domonic Raab could not take it on the chin and own up to his own failures over the debacle which was the withdrawal from Afghanistan. Instead he neatly side-steps allowing civil servant Sir Philip Barton to absorb the shrapnel. What a contrast to 1982, when Thatcher's Foreign Secretary, Lord Carrington, resigned over the invasion of the Falklands, he said that he had misread the intention of the Argentinean's, He had been at work at the time with his attention focused and not on his holidays!

All of the above and, unbelievably, 'The National' reported this morning that Sir. John Curtis said 'Yes for Independence' is only at 45%. Hey that is a better start than we had for 2014! You do also have to ask why the UK Government are so afraid to publish the data from the polling they undertook but dear Tommy Sheppard has rattled that cage so hard the UK Government are employing a 'mega-bucks' lawyer, James Eadie, to keep the data safely locked away!

A vote given to any Tory candidate is a vote that in some way supports a horde of despicable behaviour and is a vote of confidence in a barrel full of legislation that, by and large, is unhelpful to the people of Scotland.

If you are Scottish you have a chance every time you vote to change Scotland's destiny for better or for the worse. A vote for the Tories is vote for more embarrassment at the hands of Johnson and colleagues. You can use your vote to make it clear that we The Scottish People, expect the highest of standards from those whom we elect to govern us.

PB

So be engaged be interested, for there is an abyss before us. Most Scots understand that if our country does well we can all do well. Life should be more than a game where the individual who gains the most wins. I think it should be that our whole society does well so we all do well.

Denis Waitley

The greatest gifts you can give your children are the roots of responsibility and the wings of independence

Is confidence vote yet another manipulation of the system by Boris Johnson?

Also published in 'The National' 06 June 2022 22

Credit to the 54 or more Tory MP's who have at last bought about the vote of no confidence in Johnson's role as Prime Minister of the UK.

We must live in hope and in fear today as the UK is at a very dangerous moment.

If the Tory MP's, today do not take a proper stand against the way the UK Government is currently run. Johnson's position will become even stronger.

Scotland and the rest of the UK will be pulled even deeper into a world where nuclear bombs are prioritised, international laws are broken, where codes of ethics can be changed with not a moments notice, where wrong doing with in Government matters little and the friends of the Tory party gain more and more riches.

Scotland, as has been the case for decades, is once again at the mercy of Tory MP's, currently 359 of them. Six of these were voted into office by Scottish voters. As much as I want Scotland to be an Independent country I do understand that in the last Westminster election 25.1% of votes cast here in Scotland were for the Conservatives, 18.6% for Labour and

144 Cher Bonfis

9.5% for the Liberal Democrats. 53.2% of votes went to Union supporting parties. With 46% for the Independence supporters in the SNP and the Greens. Sadly 31.9% of Scottish Voters failed to express their opinion.

A vote of confidence in Mr. Johnson could cement him in his role for decades to come, a vote of no confidence might just change the direction of current travel.

It is my opinion that if Johnson wins today his position will be so strong he could very well remain in it for life. Indeed something in my head wonders if this situation, of the no confidence vote, is yet another manipulation of the system to achieve exactly that outcome.

Our referendum will be next year, we must travel the highways and byways with the message of hope for a better future for the people of Scotland, if we only stand up for ourselves and have the confidence to say we choose a better way.

Susan B Anthony

Independence is Happiness

PB

Boris Johnson will feel safe and secure after 211 Tory MPs endorsed him

Also published in 'The National' 09 June 2022 23

211 Tory MP's agree that:- Telling lies in parliament is OK. Holding parties whilst people were dying of Covid is OK. That increasing the nuclear warheads stockpile in Faslane from 180 to 260 is OK. The rape clause is OK. The bedroom tax is OK. The Internal Market Bill Act, which is a 'power-grab' against our Scottish Parliament is OK. Ignoring the United Nations over Diago Garcia is OK. Shrinking trade with the rest of the world is OK. The trade deals with the rest of the world, which were to be so abundant once the UK left the European Union, have not been so forthcoming is OK. That the NHS is not getting an extra £350 million a week is OK. That the Northern Ireland Protocol can be unilaterally tinkered with is OK. Scottish fisheries and farming have been damaged and that is OK. That the shortage of workers caused by Brexit will workout, maybe sometime in the future and that is OK. Oh and let us not forget the success (not) of Brexit is OK. Inflation of 9-10-11% is OK. That fuel prices approaching £2.00 per litre is OK. The icing on the cake…..the return to Imperial Measurements, oh that is OK….etc.

Johnson will be cock-a-hoop over his win in the vote of confidence, he will now be feeling safe and secure. Even if the by-elections go badly no one can challenge him again for one year. Johnson is not like those who came before him. I heard someone say that he would leave the Prime Minister's job soon anyway because there was not enough money in it. Then I remembered that Winston Churchill was not great with money, the 'Tory Club' had to make sure he was not thrown out of his house, Chartwell, and that he could remain there for the rest of his days. Money is not the issue, it is the 'Power' and maybe that is something admired by his wife as well. This in my opinion is not what went on with Mrs. May or Mr. Major with them the 'vote of no confidence' wounded them. Commentators keep repeating that 148 MP's voting against him has damaged him. I am certain that he will consider it a badge of merit and find ways to spin what many would consider negative, into a shining spotlight into which he will step into and do his next tap dance.

I had a conversation with someone this morning who told me I should forget about all the 'Party-Gate', they said it was 'nothing', they said 'I should be thanking Johnson for the £400 off the heating bills and admire him for giving weapons to Ukraine'. The 25% windfall tax on the energy producers is mitigated by the tax relief on increases in production from the North Sea. In 1994 the UK gave Ukraine 'Security Guarantees'. Sadly the person I was speaking with found it difficult to understand how these stories intermingle. That is a phenomenon which I often come across. It is also one of the reasons I keep writing, trying to draw ideas together and to explore how things join up.

All that logic, and more, will not turn the heads of staunch Unionists but I hope against hope it charges the emotional batteries of every Independence supporting Scot. It is our emotional response which will ultimately lead to our Independence. It really is time to talk with all our fellow Scots and for us to get really emotional about our own personal reasons for wanting Scotland's freedom.

Ho Chi Minh

Nothing is more precious than
independence and liberty

It was chilling to hear the PM tell Angela Eagle nothing can stop him now

Also published in 'The National' 13 June 2022 24

The most chilling, frightening statement from Boris Johnson yet. When he barked back, in what his Eton masters may have called impertinent, rude, or insolent, at Angela Eagle in Westminster. This incident after 41% of his MP's failed to support him in the vote of no confidence. Johnson said this....... "absolutely nothing and no one, least of all her, is going to stop us with getting on with delivering for the British people". The chilling bits...."Absolutely nothing and no one.....is going to stop us."

If you followed others of my letters you might be thinking 'oh here we go again' but this is yet another step down a staircase to a dungeon. An insidious creep in the direction that the brilliant Mhairi Black described on 28 May 2022.

Consider these things:- peaceful protest can now turn into a criminal record, via the 'Policing Bill', this Bill also affects the Traveller community. The UK Government now control the 'Independent Electoral Commission', so it needs a new name 'The Less Independent Electoral Commission'. 'The Elections Bill' requires voters to present ID to polling staff and the UK Government can decide what counts as 'fair campaigning'. In recent time the UK Government have stripped people of their citizenship, easier now because of their 'Nationality and

Borders Bill'. 'The Brexit Freedoms Bill' will remove the 1998 'Human Rights Act' from the statutes. Recently our Holyrood Parliament passed the 'United Nations Convention on the Rights of the Child Bill' into Scottish Law. (The UK Government has been under obligation, in International Law, to comply with this since 1991, but they have not.) The UK Government took us to The Supreme Court, where it was decided that some sections of the bill are outside the legislative competence of the Scottish Parliament. All of this has shades of legislative roads taken during the 1930's and when Johnson supporters blame different groups of people for the problems all of us are dragged deeper.

The UK Government is sliding around on thin ice like a skating champion with crutches. As predicted the mess of Brexit is diminishing the standards of living of us all. Workers are in the panic inflation causes. So unions threaten strike action, they know worker supply is short, commodities and consumer goods have been choked off. The government blame the Pandemic and the war in Ukraine. Blame is a word than never sits comfortably with me but if we are looking for 'Scapegoats' those who support the 211 Tory MP's who said they have confidence in Johnson, could be a place to start.

All this and more causes challenges for Kate Forbes, our Finance Minister, who yet again has to explain to Conservative MSP's, that the Scottish Government cannot have debt. We give Westminster a muckle of revenue and they return a wee bit for us to survive off. Whilst various news reporters try to evoke the idea that Nicola Sturgeon and Kate Forbes drive the trains and empty rubbish bins when they knock off from Holyrood each evening.

Then there are the cursory comments about inflation in the rest of the world and how things are just as bad, if not worse, over in 'they foreign bits'. I noticed a 'Tweet' from Ruth Richie 28 May, a litre of petrol then was just under £1.70 from a supermarket here, Ruth was sunning herself in the Canary Islands where the same amount of fuel was £1.40. In the 'Tweet' Ruth reminded that the Islands have to import all, yet here in Scotland, with a sea full of the stuff ....I had to paid £1.98 a couple of days ago.

The UK has no way out of this spiral, there is no way back to European Union. The Tory Government dragging back the failures of Margaret Thatcher and the sale of council houses, the policy which it could be argued has caused much homelessness.

Ncuti Gatwa, the fine Scottish Actor, who was born in Rwanda, but who's family fled from the 1994 genocide when he was just two years old, will climb aboard the Tardis and a great future as the new 'Doctor Who', just as Priti Patel starts sending asylum seekers, to Rwanda. At the same time, or maybe a different time altogether, Boris Johnson and co continue to travel back in time.

For anyone who is in favour of this is the surreal, dystopian set up, I will mix the sci-fi, Scotland is about to move onward and upward away from the chaos and to a future of Independence, 'make it so'.

Gaston Miron

As long as (our) independence is not achieved, it remains to be achieved

QED
Social Media Post 2022

I am sorry to be at you again so soon but it has been playing in my mind so I have to write it down.

Grant Shapps, currently 'The Transport Secretary' for the English Government. Fortunately Scotland has it's own one of these, Jenny Gilruth. However this story is our problem too and 'The Johnson Mob' failed to inform our Government about it's intentions, as has become the normal.

It goes like this. Johnson and his gang 'got Brexit done'. In the process they have fundamentally altered the economics of the UK. In the run up to the Brexit referendum no end of people predicted that the living standards for everyone in the UK would be lowered by leaving Europe. Michael Russell and Nicola Sturgeon tried to tell people that Brexit would have consequences, many of which could not be mitigated.

So here we are at the beginning of the consequences normal folk really feel. The song goes like this...The way everyone gets poorer is this prices go up and wages do not follow. 'The Bank of England' has one responsibility delegated by the treasury that is to control inflation at around 2% or write to the Chancellor and explain the failure. In our oh so sophisticated world the two things the BofE can do to achieve this are to alter interest rates up or down. Currently it is raising them, making borrowed money more expensive and that makes everything else more expensive. The BofE, any Central Bank, can issue as many bonds as it likes and, therefore, make all the money it wants, however, 'too much money chasing too few goods and services', as my economics lecturer would say, equals inflation and like many other traits recently, the various new laws enacted, give us an echo from the 1930's.

Workers are worried sick, they have rents, mortgages, and food to buy. Their children have so many needs and filling up the car, heating the house and which is the cheapest supermarket this week? So the Unions fire up, they have a purpose and a cause once more. Strike action is threatened as the offered pay rises fail to equal the inflation rate.

Shapps speaks up and says "We will repeal the nonsensical restrictions banning employers from hiring agency staff (if you can find any who are at least vaguely qualified) to provide essential cover during strikes."

In Cumnock Keir James Hardie is laid to rest, founder of the Labour party, if he is looking down from his cloud he must be wondering whatever happened to his movement and is asking why Keir Starmer's troupes, sorry troops, are not storming 10 Downing Street as you read this? I will not be using P&O Ferries again. Put my life into the hands of agency staff to sail me across the sea? Shapps continued "This country must not be held to ransom...the public must be protected." He suggested 'Marxists' are determined to turn this into a fight. It is nothing to do with Marx, it is ordinary women and men wishing to maintain what they have worked for. Even if they were taken in by Brexiteers and were misguided enough to vote for it, now the chickens are home to roost. Unions, before Thatcher, not only looked out for the pay and conditions but also helped to maintain the standards of craftsmanship within professions. The UK decided long ago that 'just about anyone can train to have a go at anything and it will do'. It took my Granddad years as apprentice to become a 'Master Craftsman', check out the tiling and plumbing in most public loos and you will know just how low standards have fallen.

Schapps and his buddies have this wrong, it is not about employment law. This is the tectonic plates of the UK economic situation shifting. This is the beginning of a huge wail and much greeting, as the UK crashes into the second, third or even forth division of the worlds economies, Already growth has slowed to the bottom of the G20 list just above Russia. So the UK may loose it's place in the G20 and the G7 and it will be working folk who will feel the chill as per usual.

If you think the Johnson Government will stop with the agency staff laws, think again. Before long there will be yet more legislation to extract whatever teeth unions may still have. If the rail unions are not yours and you have been cheesed off with the rail service recently, it could be your union next. If you know anyone struggling with the economic argument for Independence. Quod erat demonstrandum Mr. Johnson!

PB

Numbers
Social Media Story 2021

Money is numbers. Numbers are easy, in comparison to everything else. Breaking the world into numbers makes it easy for the gormless to appear clever. The way society is currently set up means that things are run by numbers. What is the best song this week? It is the one that sold the most copies. Me I cannot listen to it drives me insane! The person who earns the most money is the most successful, but his daughter hates him and his wife is having an affaire. We check the fastest, the tallest, we note the smallest and we kill ninety percent of household germs; shame it is the one percent that will kill you! More is better and so the ones who understand numbers add one and one and come up with twelve. They get to be the most successful for they learn to manipulate the numbers and cheat. Think of something you purchased a couple of years ago, something that you think was good value, without checking your old receipts. How much did you pay for it? Generally speaking we forget the money cost but we remember the quality and did it do what we wanted it to. What I am trying to say is that we are fooled by numbers, Numbers do add up and they are easy, they can easily be manipulated. The numbers game leads Government's to see in macro. If they can reduce the burden of social security by ten percent, wow they did well, however at the micro end of that equation their saving just dumped one hundred thousand people into poverty and because the books must balance. Guess what? Next months crime statistics show a ten percent rise in robberies. So now a whole lot of other folks are suffering too for they had their house burgled. People need people, they need love, they need to be valued, feel that they have value and that they are worth it. Well that is what they say on that advertisement for, I cannot remember the product, but I am worth it, my mummy told me so. You cannot put that in numerical terms.

Stephen Covey

True independence of character empowers us to act rather than be acted upon

Independence and Monarchy
Social Media Post 2022

It really matters not if it is cold or it is hot, if it is dry or it is wet, if it is night or it is day, summer or winter, autumn or spring. You turn on the television news and see the reporters line up a bunch of folk who oppose whatever condition appertains during the past hours.

Where I stay most of the folk who live near me are supporters of the Union, they were jubilant over the Queen Elizabeth's platinum event, they had their wee Union Flag bunting and portraits of the Queen. God bless her too, if you have to have a Queen, Elizabeth has done her best to keep the show on the road. I am not for the Monarchy for reasons we have not space for here, may be another time.

I blether with all my neighbours, despite them backing the Union, they are all good people and we all get along. Of course I bought up the subject of IndyRef2 after the announcement this week. To a man and woman the response was 'We have always been in the Union, that's the way it should be.' Then they went on to tell me how terrible things are, inflation, and this should be better, and that should be better, and about the awful mess of the current Tory Government. So I gently suggest that maybe if we changed the way we are governed we could change all of the problems and make things better. We then get stuck in a feed-back loop. I think because they live in a 'Comfort Zone' of what they have always known. It is always much easier to stay where you are than risk a change. I will add the caveat that we are a group of folk who are all long in the tooth.

There were a lot of middle age, middle class, middle England Tories on the news this evening. It was actually all to much for me. I had listened to some moaning minis complaining that it was too hot in England, it has been blowing a hoolie all week here, whilst in the background there were people splashing about in the sea my mind flitted to the discussions about sewage dumped in rivers but I decided to leave that thought where it was. The hot weather did not deter the Tory men, in their suits and ties, pontificating, voicing support for their leader, even though he had let them down by jetting off to Ukraine to once more avoid the appointment he had made with them. It has been the same all though my life, generation after generation of the Tory elite thinking they and they alone are anointed to govern the rest of us. With the minions, their voters, kneeling down and accepting the status quo. I don't like it, I never have.

What I like is the progressive, forward thinking, excitement of the Government we have elected time and again in Scotland. Oh yes I have heard the reporters on the news picking out the nuggets they have found to hold up as fault in what our government has done, or what they claim they have not done. I have heard people around here complain about the SNHS yet I have seen ambulances arrive in the night to come to several peoples aid and I have taken some of them to doctors appointments in my car. They all got jagged for Covid. I say to them that the UK is not like everywhere else in the world, other people in other countries do things differently and often the outcomes are superior, one neighbour said 'well I only have your word for that'. I say if you want things to change you have to change some things.

They say we love the Queen, I say that is a different issue from the Independence situation. They say what about friends and family in England and I tell of the 'Common Travel Area' that has been in working fully since 1925 and ask why would that change? They say they never heard of it. I also inform them that there are trade barriers between the VAT free Channel Islands and the rUK and that the UK Border Force carry out customs checks, so that thing about there being an economic border from Berwick to the Solway, well bring it on. Strange how the Northern Irish Unionists are so upset by a border that has actually made them richer.

I will keep chipping at the folk around here. If the news reporters turned up here I would hide. I know though they would more than likely pick on my fellows to interview after all their opinion is the total opposite of mine. I better buy a tube of sun lotion just in case that old sun makes an appearance before the end of August. Roll on October 2023.

Cher Bonfis

Propaganda
Social Media Post 2022

Congregatio de Propaganda Fide was created in 1622 by the Roman Catholic Church during their fight back from Jean Calvin's Reformation 60 years before. 60 years before that The Holy Roman Emperor Maximilian 1 is said to have been the first to use the printing press for propaganda purposes. If you go to Geneva, in Switzerland, the four great figures of the reformation are immortalised in statue form Guillaume Farel, Jean Calvin, Theodore de Beze, John Knox. John Knox bought the reformation from Switzerland to Scotland. Around the time of Mary Queen of Scots. You can still feel his influence today. He was a master of propaganda. Over the following 400 years propaganda has developed into a form of art. It is so very difficult to distinguish between news and that which is merely a story to redirect the minds of members of the general public. I try to get around the propaganda by reading the news from different publications and how the same stories are presented in other countries.

Many people know the word propaganda from the time when the Nazi Party controlled Germany in the 1930's. Joseph Goebbels was the head of The Ministry of Public Enlightenment and Propaganda. Many people will be familiar with George Orwell's book 1984 and Aldous Huxley's Brave New World. There are many other such works.

Today the television and radio and internet provide such powerful tools to those who desire to influence us the ordinary women and men, the workers, the servers, those of us who have not put ourselves forward to grasp the position of President or Prime Minister.

Most of the folk who read this will be people who would substitute the word British for English before the words Broadcasting Corporation. This evening Channel 4 news came over as the UK Government's very own mouth piece. An economist declined to point out that Brexit is the outstanding factor which distinguishes the UK economy as the one with the highest inflation and the lowest growth. Then John Redwood made an appearance, in his uncompromisingly depressing way, alongside another younger 'economist', who half mentioned that Brexit might have been playing a small part in the hauless, glaikit, muckle, raivel (clumsy, stupid, big, muddle) we are all now in.

It seems that none can see that trying to propaganda a way out of the strikes will not work. The truth is that a lot of people in the UK who accepted David Cameron's call for a referendum on European Union Membership and enough of them voted to leave it, mostly because of the propaganda presented by Boris Johnson and Dominic Cummings. The adjustment has now started to happen, each and everyone of us living in the UK is now experiencing the beginning of a downward adjustment in our standard of living. Prices will rise and incomes will not rise enough to catch up the difference. I can understand why the unions are finding their old strengths again, it is kind of 'comforting' to hear union leaders emulating Peter Sellers in 'I'm All Right Jack', the film from 1959. However, this is going to be a long hull, union leaders may well secure a pay rise but they will need another not to far along the track, because democracy provided Brexit and on top of it democracy provided a UK Government further to the right of politics then ever before in the UK. It really is time to move from propaganda to reality.

It is probable that if you are reading this you support the idea of an Independent Scotland. We have now 16 months to help any 'No's' and 'Don't Know's' to feel that Scotland would be far, far better off as independent nation within the European Union, the glare of the propaganda is one of the biggest challenges in this struggle we must undertake.

I think we should also make policy now, that within the new version of our country, we should have a public broadcaster, a newspaper and some Internet media, which cannot be controlled by any Government which is running our country, nor multi-millionaires, or corporations. I would put forward the idea that every citizen of our Scotland should be an equal shareholders of this body. It should have written within it's charter that it must never be the mouthpiece of propaganda. Nation should speak peace to nation and as John Reith, a

Scottish Calvinist, from the beautiful town of Stonehaven, suggested it should Inform, Educate and Entertain.

Jim Rohn

It's not dependency that creates your future.
It's independence that creates your better future.

Cher Bonfis

Back in the Good Old Days
Social Media Post 2022

Back in the good old days, when I travelled far and wide over the continent of Europe, there was a bit of hassle when passports were checked at borders. There was money changing too, Dutch Guilder's, German Marks, Francs-Belgium-French-Luxemburg-Swiss, Austrian Shillings, Italian Lira, Spanish Pesetas. Generally speaking things moved quite well. Then things got better, the Euro and Schengen and suddenly the route from Stockholm to Málaga, with a fair wind, was possible without border police. To me at that time this was marvellous. After my trips the coming home meant meeting customs officials and passport control of the UK. If I returned via a port in the South of England there could be 500 miles before I could get some real Scottish pounds for my Euro's. The looks from the passport and customs people often made me feel as if I had committed a crime, the question 'where are you going?' used to bug me, as if it were any of their business.

Just six years ago you and I were citizens of the largest free trading area, we had the right to travel, study, live and work in 27 other lands (a few more if you break the UK into it's parts and add Switzerland). To me that was amazing and I took advantage of the opportunity that it provided. In those days I had business from Catania to Durness. I could see the smoke rising from mount Etna and a couple of days later be looking out from the cliff tops to Sango Bay.

It was not only me, many people I knew harvested a bounty in rewards, career, money and personal. I think now how fortunate I have been to have been a part of that. I could never understand why anyone would not want a bit of it for themselves. It seemed to me that Ted Heath sold the EEC to the UK as an economic club but even at that time the ambition of other European nations was far more than just that, many who fought against membership wanted it just as a money club forever. Thatcher seemed to think that those 'nasty Germans' wanted to be in charge of it all and she remembered the war so she shouted no, no, no. Then John Major tried to expand the UK into the Maastricht Treaty and had one hell of a time from the Euro-Sceptics. It always seemed to me that for the UK the European Union was something that was done unto us, rather than the UK being a part of the powerhouse to move it forward to make better lives for all citizens.

This is just to remind you that we lost a lot when Cameron held the Brexit referendum and then scurried of like a half drowned rat leaving us in the sewer of incompetent Brexit negotiators. Then onto the current state of affaires in the strange island of Westminster, where *bon-bons play on the sunny beach of peppermint bay*, I don't think.

Now we can feel the icy waters rising around our feet and the true costs of all the folly are becoming clearer than a big red bus, this is to remind you that, depending on how you do your maths, each person in the UK contributed around about 35 pence per day to belong to the European Union, and in return for that membership we received so much, I could start writing the list but it would take a long while. That is not even £120 per year. What does a gym, or golf, membership set you back each year?

I read a press release this morning, it pointed out yet another of the consequences of Brexit. From May 2023 any Scottish person wishing to go to a European Union member state will have to apply to European Travel Information and Authorisation System and under go security checks. There will be a charge made of £6.00 per person, and trips are limited to 90 days. Suppose you are a Mum, Dad and two children family that is yet another £24.00 to find, when we were a part of the EU you would not have noticed the 35 pence a day the UK Government paid the bill out of it's income and borrowing so your contribution was made through your taxes.

Some of my friends and some of my family members voted leave, I will still love them but I will never forgive them for the part they played in stripping me of my citizenship and all the benefits it accrued to me. I live in hope that I will still be alive when Scotland becomes independent and I get a Scottish Passport which I will not need to show to passport control as we once again become members of the EU, in all those places on the continent of Europe that I love so much and then return home here to Scotland without the chill of the UK Border Force as a welcome.

PB

Not Everyone Agrees with Me
Social Media Post 2022

You may find it hard to credit but not everyone agrees with the things I write! There are some folk who think that I do not already know that!

I wrote the above piece last night and this morning there is a notice from James claiming that my article is 'Simply Propaganda'.

Interestingly I then opened my email client and looked through the messages, I get press releases from various organisations, the one I am looking at quotes a study by 'The Resolution Foundation' and 'The London School of Economics'. This study highlights the DEVASTATING impact of Brexit. Lower wages, reduced productivity and a shrinking economy. The study concludes that Brexit is making the UK poorer and we will see further reduction in productivity and wages over the coming decade.

In September 2010 Cardinal Walter Kasper, of the Vatican, quipped, in an interview for a German Magazine, that arriving at Heathrow Airport was like landing in a third world country.

Several times yesterday I saw an article in Facebook streams that many young English people exhibit the least literacy in the developed world, this is not a new story, the OECD have reported similar year on year over the past decade.

PB

In 1696 the Scottish parliament passed the 'Act for Setting Schools' it established a school for every parish in Scotland. By 1750 most Scottish towns had a public lending library, Scotland was the most literate country in Europe. Ordinary working people could, and did, read the works of Adam Smith and David Hume. Our current Scottish Government have invested heavily in our schools, over 1000 have been built or upgraded.

One question to ask the 'No's' and the 'Don't Knows' is in which society would they prefer to take their chances.

Maria Montessori

The essence of independence is to be able to do something for one's self

It's the Economy
Social Media Post 2022

"I t's the economy stupid" said James Carville in 1992 to get Bill Clinton elected as President of the USA. The statement made it easy, it made it all about money and numbers. Money and numbers are easy because humans invented them. Unlike human relationships and emotions, which have no magic formula and can go off at any tangent at any moment. Money has only to balance in the accounts. That though leaves a question mark by Carville's statement 'What is the economy?' The answer is that it is you and me and all our fellow humans spending, investing, borrowing, saving, giving, banking, gambling, taking and losing the stuff we call money. Money needs a makeover. We can see that others feel the same way, they have invented crypto-currencies and these have now been pulled into the main-stream as the European Union have begun to regulate them and El Salvador has adopted crypto currency Bit Coin as legal tender. A short time ago 'The National' offered all subscribers 1000 Scot Coin, so I have a wallet of that amount. However I am not wishing to go further along that road today. What this is about is the value of each of us, because we are the economy stupid.

I have spent my life in a running battle with many of my fellows over the value of the human being. I have done my best to appreciate all those with whom I come into contact.

PB

Even those who have done great harm or wrong to me. I have tried to see their side of the story and I have tried to see what I could learn by whatever experience I was involved in. I will not claim that I have always achieved a betterment of myself, there are things which I can neither forgive or forget, some will no doubt say that it is necessary to forgive as otherwise the healing cannot begin, well open wounds have their place and maybe they help, at times, by way of reminding not to spring the same traps again. I try to value my fellows whatever they have to offer.

In motivational books it can be read that of all the millions of sperm it only took one to fertilise the egg so you were a winner before you were born. So that makes all 108 billion people, who have ever lived (Figure from the World Atlas), winners. In my keepsakes cupboard I have an ornament I have owned since 1983. A servant who worked in a house of a wealthy man I was a guest of in Indonesia and I struck up a friendship, she invited me to her home. It was a long journey through Jakarta to her, modest, slum, dwelling. I will never forget the warmth of the greeting from her and her friends and family. I looked about to find nice things to say and I picked out the ornament, not really because I thought it was wonderful but among the chaos it was a focal point. A few weeks later, at home here in Scotland, to my horror, a package arrived containing the ornament with a note thanking me for my visit offering the ornament as a gift to remember the day by. This family had nothing of material value and she worked for a man who was privileged beyond my resources and in ways she could never reach without a South China Sea worth of luck. The model of society where the few having so much and the many have so little to me is repugnant but I am one small person of the 8 billion folk currently inhabiting earth. I also know I always had more of a share than my servant friend.

In sociology lectures of college days the formula was simple if you are poor you are worse off in just about everyway. I think it is great to be Scottish under the current Government who by design, or accident, seem to have grasped the idea that poverty is where the harm is. More than that they, I think, are trying to pull a generation out of poverty.

1 Improvements to maternity and neonatal care. 2 Free vitamins for all who are pregnant. 3 The Scottish Milk and Snack Scheme, 4 Maternal and infant Nutrition survey. 5 Giving all an equal start with the Baby Box. 6 £20.00 per week per child the child payment. 7 30 hours a week free early learning and childcare. 8 Medicines free of charge. 9 SNHS free of charge. 10 1000 improved and new school buildings and free education. 11 Efforts made to increase the numbers of teachers (not an easy task).

At First Ministers questions a favourite of the opposition parties is the one about the so called 'attainment gap', I am never quite sure about that but if all of the things in the above list, along with all the other things that are being done here in

Scotland can carry on there is a good chance we could raise an entire generation and, hopefully, rid our society of so many of the things which make one human think that they are better than another. All in all that would in itself improve the economic performance of our country. However what is more to the point, it seems to me, it is a statement that Scottish Society values each citizen and aspires to offer them all the best start in life. I am sure that within the current constitutional arrangement it will be more difficult to improve. I am certain that with Independence we will be in a better position to do more and it will make all our lives better. Money and numbers will convince few, emotions will sway the many.

Albert Einstein

For me a simple message, to think and act with courage, independence and imagination

Bi-Coloured-Python-Rock-Snake
Social Media Post 2022

Before being a spouse and a parent, before computers and internet, I could generate more money than it cost me to live (oh for a Tardis). Then I belonged to the 'Folio Society', they produced beautiful books. Extravagance, I freely admit, the books offered could be purchased cheaply from John Menzies, but I liked the box covers and the illustrations, the smell as they acquired age. I have given so many books away, some I wish I had kept but I still have many. Among those from the 'Folio Society' is Rudyard Kipling's 'Just So Stories'. I do not want to have a 'woke' debate about Rudyard and the society in which he lived. This is to draw your attention to a few lines of prose from 'The Elephant's Child'. 'The Just So Stories' came about when Kipling's children told him to stop 'polishing' the stories to make them 'better' they said leave them as they were 'just so'.

Many will know the story, here is a brief précis. Long ago elephants had a short nose, the elephants child travelled far to find out what Crocodiles eat for dinner. On the bank of the Limpopo river he found a Crocodile who grabbed his nose in it's teeth and started to pull. A Python came to the elephants aid.

"Then the Bi-Coloured-Python-Rock-Snake scuffled down from the bank and said, 'My young friend, if you do not now, immediately and instantly, pull as hard as ever you can. It is my opinion that your acquaintance in the large-pattern leather ulster' (and by this he meant the Crocodile) 'will jerk you into yonder limpid stream before you can say Jack Robinson.'

This next paragraph is a message to any Tory MP, who has a nanogram of decency and who feels that the current leadership of the UK is failing to expedite the responsibilities of governance in a proper, truthful and legal manor. If you can elect someone, or get yourself elected, to the 1922 committee and change the rules, and oust Boris Johnson from his position as the leader of your party, do it. If you do not 'oh best beloved': and the Bi-Coloured-Python-Rock-Snake continued *'yonder self-propelling man-of-war with the upper-plated upper deck will permanently vitiate your future career.'*

Johnson is unlike his predecessors. If he wins this round, of this battle, he will be even more entrenched and he will look to stay on as Prime Minister for life. Look about the world and see the dictatorships that many millions of people currently live in. Is this what people here really want? We live in a so-called democracy, so I accept the outcomes of elections and referendums when I disagree with the result. Dictatorships usually remove democratic rights, this has already begun to happen here.

One often hears it said that Johnson is the 'Recruiting Sergeant for Independence', I think there is strength in that argument but if he is allowed to more strongly secure his position and to remain in that position, ultimately it will make it more difficult, or even impossible, for us to breakaway.

The UK is in peril, which is another way of saying that you and I, fellow Scots, are in grave danger. The folly of Brexit has many more manifestations yet to come. We still have the hope of being a free and independent Scotland. It is imperative that we spend our time now concentrated on that dream. Unionists must be helped to understand that the United Kingdom they still long to be apart of has gone. The more that Johnson and his supporters continue to run the show the less that old fashioned vision of the UK will be. The UK is abandoning the Union Jack, to the rear of sea going vessels, and Admiral Johnson has hoisted the 'Skull and Cross Bones', this is what it seems like to many of our international neighbours. Citizens supporting this regime are giving approval to lying, law breaking and changing story narratives without the batting of an eye.

It is not good enough to leave the story 'Just So'. We must pull, and pull, and pull. Johnson will thrash his tail like an oar in the water but we must pull harder, until we hear the 'plop up and down the Limpopo' as his grip gives way. After, that, we will have changed, like the elephant we will have a new nose and we will be able to do new and extraordinary things.

Cher Bonfis

Things will not be the same after independence, they will be new and full of the possibilities that are now buried by the Act of Union. We cannot leave things 'just so' we must change and make things better.

Mahatma Gandhi

To safeguard democracy the people must have a
keen sense of independence,
self respect and their oneness

Conservative leadership contest shows how far to the right the UK has gone

Also published in 'The National' 20 July 2022 25

One of my Face Book pals always signs off *'You know the story never trust a Tory. Lang Mae Yer Lum Reek'.* I have never, could never, will never vote Conservative. All my adult life the Tory's have been going further to the right in politics and that is not where I think the world should go. I can see how the free market has it's place but it does not and cannot solve all of human-kind problems. Left to it's own devices the free market produces the 'haves' and the 'have-nots'. In the utopia I live in my head the society does well and so everyone does well. I think that that kind of idea goes down well with many of my fellow Scots. Not all of them but I am only looking of a majority. I think an Independent Scotland could be the ideal growing ground for my Utopia.

We have to become an Independent country. If you have not yet worked that out look at the choice of candidates for a new Prime Minister of the dis-United Kingdom. You can see from that list how far to the right things have gone. The candidates reflect the view of the Conservative MP's currently elected to the Westminster Parliament. You can see that Tom Tugendhat has had to drop out and that tells you that the 'kind of reasonable sort of Tory', if there is such a beast, is far from being in the ascendant.

Liz Truss claiming she has a record of success in making trade deals, really all that has happened is that agreements which were once apart of the benefit of being an EU member have been flipped into place as individual deals between various countries and the UK. She stood there on the TV debate echoing the clothes of Thatcher but with not a fraction of the gravitas. Remember she also spent half a million pounds hiring a plane to take, how many people was it? Fourteen? To Australia and they came back (remember that bit).

Reading around about Kemi Badenoch one might be fooled into thing she was the 'refugee made good', I am all for that but it seems that she is from a family of doctors and that she enjoyed a private education. She could have been both of these of course.

Then Penny Mordaunt to me she comes over like a school headmistress 'do it my way now and it will be fun, oh and by the way there is no other choice available'. I have it all worked out and everything has been cost-ed but I am not dealing with that now.

Then we come to the front runner. Sunak. I cannot find any warmth towards him either. I have Shakespearian characters flitting around my dendrites is the a Julius Ceasar or Macbeth or Hamlet or was he just looking for a pound of flesh? Sunak has obviously planned his move and got his publicity made before he stabbed Johnson in the back. He has got one thing going for him *he did stab Johnson in the back*. We have to ask ourselves is that really a good enough reason for putting someone in the driving seat of a cockpit of a country? The other question is if he does win this rather truncated election for the person who becomes ships-captain would it be possible to get him to live up to his assertion in 2017 that the timing of indyref2 should be pushed back until Brexit has passed.

On the positive side the UK Government's exertions to have the Supreme Court throw out the request from our Lord Advocate to examine whether our Parliament has the competence to make decisions our population voted for time and time again over the past few years. Oh just remember that those were real voters in real elections where all our registered voters in Scotland had a chance to record their choice. We voted for the party that offered a referendum on the future of our country and we elected our First Minister, all of us, OK so some people did not vote for Nicola but the majority did and that is how it works. When you hear the Tory cry we have a huge mandate, they do not -- that was Johnson's mandate, he is gone (I hope, although I still wonder if he will come back) and with him the mandate. By rights there should be a general election and the SNP should make it a one issue competition our Independence.

Cher Bonfis

New 'I' generation of leaders dismiss need for teamwork

Also published in 'The National' 31 July 2022 26

Any one looking to be elected to political office must have driving personal ambition, that is understandable, right and proper. Who needs someone in a job who would rather be elsewhere? Survival of the fittest plays a big role in such scenarios. In other professions, lets say acting, truly 'big stars' not only have personal ambition they have talent. They have learned to do things that 'ordinary folks' might think they can do but actually only with talent and experience can the 'big stars' achieve fetes of the impossible. I can attest from my involvement that the majority of successful actors are humble, generous and appreciative of their peers. They understand that it is team work that creates great productions. Team effort pulls each new audience 'on-side' making the life of each audience member a wee bit better, even if an audience member came to a show under protest to appease a spouse, or they picked the wrong screen at the mulitplex.

Write a list of former politicians labelled 'These Politicians were not only fiercely ambitious for themselves but had the desire to make their community/town/county/country a better place for all it's inhabitants'. In Scotland I know some personally and I know others by their reputation, I think that is a wonderful thing and think that we are fortunate to have many such politicians in our Holyrood Parliament.

Looking south of our border or to the USA in recent time, there have been two horrendous examples of politicians whose driving personal ambition has had hardly a gram of concern for the welfare or betterment of the society over which they have been elected to govern. Trump's long list of catastrophes includes allowing manufacturers to dump raw effluent into the water courses of America and loading the Supreme Court with judges who's attitude towards women's freedom is hardly different to that of the Taliban in Afghanistan. Mirrored by Johnson's administration in England who relaxed rules allowing the private water companies to release raw sewage into rivers after Brexit caused shortages of the chemicals required to treat it. Now a former Speaker of the House of Lords has warned Johnson not to make many more Tory Peers. Where has this 'right' of exiting Prime Ministers to stock up the Peers come from? Like Trump Johnson has still ambition to get back to the 'top-job'. In my opinion not for the betterment of the people but purely to satisfy their insatiable desire for power.

The Tory party is demonstrating all the reasons why it should not be in power. Sunak in his over priced suits and expensive shoes (I have nothing against the shoe makers and tailors, craftsmen remarkable) but how many of us ordinary mortals can relate to the purchase of a suit price £2000+ or shoes £400+. Then there is Truss who has such a grip on gravitas that she could be floating, aye but she does have a ghost like quality. The pair of them touring about and mouthing what they think people want to hear. 'I will send more to Rwanda', 'I will stop the Chinese'. What is it with this 'I' business, when did it get to be that a Prime Minister was 'god' and what 'I' say will be done? They seem to have no idea that government should be about the people and the environment of the land they have been elected to govern. Their job is to make things better for the population as a whole, not just to make things better for their friends who run the businesses which make more and more money from the edicts of members of the cabinet.

Our Scottish government are clearly aware of their responsibility towards all citizens who reside here. They, I believe, understand that there are those of us who wish that Scotland is an Independent nation once more. It understands that some of us within this group are more impatient than are others. It also knows there are many who wish that Scotland remains in the dis-united Kingdom (in the last 70 years why has no one has changed that to Queendom!)

The stark contrast here is whilst the Tories are choosing a new leader based purely on the 'Personal Ambition' of two very weak, one might suggest talent-less candidates. Here in Scotland we have highly talented ministers and a leader who, I believe, want a better deal for all who choose to make their home here. A good government should be as a good team of theatricals working together to produce a great show that improves the lives of all our people, even if they are at the show under duress or by mistake.

Ibrahim Rugova

I want to emphasize the fact that the independence of Kosovo should and will be recognized.

Cher Bonfis

Quantum Physics
Social Media Post 2022

There are things that are difficult to understand. Quantum physics would be one for most of us. How NASA scientists interpret the data coming back from their new Webb telescope would be another of things I could not just laugh off as if I had a clue. It would seem that members of the Tory party have things that are seemingly just as difficult because they need yet another thirty days of hustings so that they can workout which of two people will 'WIN THE PRIZE', as some newspapers put it, to become prime minister of the dis-united-queendom.

Here we are in one of the most 'developed societies' the world has to offer. WiFi available on every corner. Mobile phones in the grasp of rich and homeless alike. Where the encyclopaedia of the world and it's history and that which is known about the universe, is available, in just about any language, to be absorbed by anyone who is able to read. Yet it will take the ancient workings of the Tory party an 'age' to select one of two woefully inadequate candidates to take the, so called, top job. Well they have form look at the fiasco when Rees-Mogg insisted that MP's should vote by going through the lobby's in Westminster keeping socially distanced, during the Covid Pandenmic, the queue stretched down the road outside in a pathetic display of nonsense. Surely this election is another such display, It is hardly that Sunak or Truss are giving us lectures on quantum physics or the Webb telescope, or that they are bright enough to do so. They spend all their time in the 'if I—I will' mode which shows us that this 'competition' has little to do with the four nations but has all to do with their personal ambition.

I think that is one of the big fault lines between what many of the English electorate seem to want verses what a majority of the electorate in Scotland would prefer.

Sunak claims that the Union is under real risk because of Nicola Sturgeon. He has not got the idea that Scottish people voted for Nicola Sturgeon and therefore we have asked her and our government to put to the test whether the Scottish people as a whole would now prefer to leave the Union and go our own way. Yes we know that Nicola had to be ambitious to reach the position of First Minister and to maintain that position for such a long period. We know that she is a canny lass who has a plan and is executing it. There are those within our YES FAMILY who are not her supporters, however, the majority of us do and one reason for that is because we can see that it is not her desire to remain as First Minister for the sake of it, that is her driving force. It is her desire to see the people of our country living good prosperous lives. She, you and I know that we will be in a better position to achieve that as an independent country within Europe. We also know, I have said it many times before, that Nicola is not the only leader within our movement wants that same prize.

That is what I wish to point out, the difference between self-centred 'I want to be Prime Minister' and Scotland's fight for freedom from the political contract which holds us back from providing better lives for each individual in our society. Neither Sunak nor Truss understand, well why should they none of their Tory predecessors understood either. More and more Scots see our future as an Independent country with leaders who want the best, not simply to satisfy their personal ambitions but for us the people of Scotland.

I think that is easy enough to understand. So when either of these prime minister wannerbes claim they will drive support for Indyref2 down it is best just to laugh it off as if you did not understand. We understand independence is what we want and when do we want it? ....

Wladyslaw Stanislaw Reymont

A free peasant means free Poland, for he is the foundation of her greatness and independence

Freedom to Speak
From 04 Auguist 2022

Please hear me: SPAIN: Pablo Hasel, César Strawberry. RUSSIA: Pussy Riot. USA: Jamal Knox, Mayhem Mal. ETHIOPIA: Seenaa Solomon, Elias Kiflu. The names of a few of the entertainers who have received sanction through law for their lyrics and performances. The length of such lists are often in proportion to how far to the right politics are in a particular country. The Council of Europe has condemned Spain for violating 'freedom of expression'. In the penal code of Spain it is written that expression is 'a right of crucial importance for a free and pluralistic public debate'. However, that does not seem to mean much to the authorities in this European country.

I would count myself as a 'left-winger' for want of a better shorthand. The problem with the groups on my side of the spectrum is that we allow and encourage debate, we offer platforms for our opponents and we are often gracious enough to listen to what they have to say. Sadly, it seems to me, often the 'right-wingers' have a wish to shut down debate and put that which fails to chime with their view of the world into prison.

Until yesterday I had not been alarmed at what was coming from the Tory Party leadership candidates. The way I see it the pair are trying to step into shoes which are way to big for them. Then I saw an article in The National, repeated on the front cover today and my blood felt cold within me. I can see how far to the right England has gone and I know some people in Scotland who admire that. I read of Sunak's comments in absolute horror. I thought 'how many more missives to The National are left for me to write, as under Sunak's proposal I am surely for the high-jump. Of course I would not be the first author to suffer because of a narrow framing of a legal code. So just before I am clapped in irons let me say this. I am very happy that England is England and that they have a government which seemingly has been elected by a majority of it's electorate, ditto Wales and Northern Ireland. I am still convinced that Scotland has a different culture and a different moral stance and that the people of Scotland would be financially better off and served better by having all the leavers of power as a Sovereign Independent country. I have no hatred of anyone but who knows how my words could be twisted. Anyway I am only a small voice and maybe they will not get to me as quickly as they reach some of my more high profile fellows!

THIS IS THE QUOTE THE ALARMS ME from The National 03 August 2022: *THOSE who "vilify" Britain face being treated as extremists and referred for deradicalisation under new plans from Tory leadership hopeful Rishi Sunak. The former chancellor intends to change the definition of extremism to allow people with an "extreme hatred of Britain" to be put through the Prevent Programme.*

Maybe I should call *Aamer Anwar* now because if my above statement does not get me FaceBook and The National undoubtedly has a memory of something that will. The further to the right politics shifts the fewer rights people have. I have nothing but respect for the rights of all my fellow humans. I may disagree and not like what they say or do but I have a big problem when I feel that things are moving to shut off my voice, my opinion and my right to express my view. 'We should ignore Nicola Sturgeon' said Truss. How is that any different from putting rappers in jail so that their voices can no longer be heard?

My great grandparents, grand parents and parents were all involved in World War I and II, they and millions of others suffered the agony of war for the freedom I have enjoyed all my life. The right wing hooligans who have pulled Scotland from the European Union, which kept the peace for seventy years, seem to have no concept of what a dangerous path they ask people to follow them down. You cannot say what you please in Russia and they war with Ukraine. You cannot say what you please in China and they rattle sabres at Taiwan.

Here we are in the Brexit Cost of Living Crisis and the Tory party say: 'we do not need to listen to the unions we will change the law so agency staff can do the work instead'. I ask you is that not exactly the same thing? How long before strike action is outlawed? I learned in sales training 'you have one mouth and two ears' use these wonders in the same proportion.

David Wooster

I am dying, but with a strong hope and persuasion that my country will gain her independence.

Brexit remains the unspoken reason for so much of our economic pain

Also published in 'The National' 14 August 2022 27

My task was to be in charge of 40 teenagers and get them to present a musical play that they had written, to their parents, at the end of a summer school. They did pretty well, there was a great musician, sadly deceased, who helped them with the music, you would know of him if I wrote his name but I will not. The parents were very impressed by the actual performance as were the powers who were in charge of the course. However there had been a hiccup after the dress rehearsal. The course director sat in and watched that afternoon. He said nothing as he left the theatre but in the evening I received a note summoning me, the musician, and helpers to his office. Around the large table and he tore into me, the 'director' and told me how he loathed the whole play and how disappointed he was and that he could not allow the show to be performed the following evening. He was very angry. This though was not my first day in the job and I had learned from my previous experiences that often when someone rejects 'The Whole Thing' it was actually only one little part of it that they did not like. So having paused for breath I started to ask him questions about each scene of the play. It was not long before we came to the nub of his problem. There was a scene where using the large trap door in the floor of the stage the youngsters had buried a coffin as in a funeral. As the moaners walked away one of them was heard to say of the deceased 'I did not like him anyway.' Well forty years ago we had not heard of 'woke' and I suspect today such a line would might be ill viewed. The thing was that the whole play fell down upon six words. Once identified it was easy to remove them and later my boss told me it was the best of my productions. The take-a-way is 'if you have a problem identify the cause'.

I am sure like many others who hold the cause of Scottish Independence deep in our hearts we watch the Truss/Sunak debacle with a certain amount of glee thinking they said Johnson was a recruiting sergeant for Independence 'look at these two'! "I WILL", "I WILL", "I WANT", "I WANT", I, I, I, I. There is a *Neil Diamond* song 'We'…. *'Love is all about chemistry Isn't something you go off to school to learn It isn't math or ancient history It's the kind of thing that comes down to simple terms It's not about you It's not about me Love is all about WE'.* The Tory party leadership is not about 'WE the four nations of the UK' it is all about "I want to be Prime Minister, because I know what is best for everyone!"

From all I have seen these past days Truss of Sunak have yet to identify the problem and even if they do the inhabitants of the 'British Isles' are doomed to a down grade in their living standards and a winding back of the clocks to far greater numbers of the population living in destitution.

I read on 5 August that the Swiss were concerned that their inflation rate had risen 3.4% over the year to July. According to 'Trading Economics' the UK is 9.4% lower than Turkey at 79.6% and lower than some other European countries. The projection from the Bank of England is 13% with interest rates rising along side. The UK has other problems which are not easily cured the Tory government have managed to choke off the supply of labour and goods. There has been a good deal of cash wafting around from furlough. Despite Scottish seas still being full of oil and our hills being full of wind the global energy market is under pressure from the war. I am still a devotee of Adam Smith of Kirkcaldy, I have written this before, 'Too much money chasing too few goods brings inflation'. Put it the other way around if there is not enough of an item to go around it's price will increase. Yes the war and the Pandemic are factors in the story but cutting the UK off from the European Single Market is the problem that will keep on giving. Truss could make trade deals with every country in Africa and combined their output each year does not match the output of France.

43 years ago I had a mortgage on a house and the interest rate rose to 15%, it was not easy but I survived. The problem for the UK is that Brexit will not go away, neither the Tory or the Labour Party want it to go away and that is going to be the continuing problem. Even Brexit Opportunities Minister Rees-Mogg has said that we might have to wait 50 years to see the benefits of Brexit. I am a Rabbie Burns fan 'rocks melt

in the sun', with climate change that is at least a possibility! The prospect of me being here in 50 years is zero. So here are three words 'Get Independence Done'.

Omar Bongo

But since independence, Gabon is one of the few countries in Central Africa that enjoys peace and stability.

Even after Boris Johnson we need new words to describe the grim reality of Liz Truss-led UK

Also published in 'The National' 27 August 2022 28

I did an internet search and found a fashion business using the slogan 'Mad about Fashion'. Meanings of words change. We sometimes need new adjectives. Over a decade from the mid 1970's I spent much time producing over four hundred entertainments within institutions that care for those with mental health issues. Words used to describe such people are often derogatory and then attributed to the world outside such places. Mad can mean 'good' as equally as it can be 'bad'. I think that a brand new set of words is required to describe the acts of people who are not ill in their minds or are confined within institutions. The people I speak of are free to wander as they please and to take up positions of high office, one I have in mind is a candidate for Prime Minister of the UK, which sadly still includes us Scotland.

There was a time when a cause of mental illness was thought to be the moon. 'Lunar', is from the Latin word for the moon. Astrologer's claimed that when our Moon, Saturn and Mars were aligned people were more likely to suffer diseases of the mind. Those who compiled King James VI's bible included the word *'lunatick'* in Matthew's gospel. It is still common to hear derogatory words attributed to those with mental illness transferred to anything that was disliked. With greater understanding change has come about, the acceptable language around mental illness has been altered through various laws, for example, in 2012, USA, 'The 21st Century Language Act' removed the word used in Matthew from all Federal Laws.

'Astronomy' and the James Webb telescope has provided beautiful photos of Jupiter, fascinating, but I have no interest in 'Astrology', however maybe heavenly bodies have been in alignment to bring a collective disorder over the past few days. Here are a few incidents I have noted:

1. Independence Day, Ukraine, Russians fired missiles at a railway station and killed and injured many. 2. French people got angry when prisoners had a go-kart race in Fresnes prison. You might disapprove but the punishment is to have liberty removed, could it be those who arranged the race know more about keeping order in prison and reforming inmates than outside observers? 3. A Scottish person told me yesterday that prison is a 'holiday camp', I asked how they knew that, there was no response. 4. Another told me 'capital punishment is the answer'. 5. Then I was told all about the racial prejudice the person held and how they had voted for Brexit because of the flood of foreigners invading Scotland. 6. Another said that SNP had 'had it's day' and is in decline, membership falling. When I gently suggested that the SNP had won the last Holyrood election and quietly asked where the information had come from the person got very upset. 7. I wrote a message to a friend and asked how their day had been a

snappy rebuff came back 'Frustrating, continual distractions', I was sorry I asked! 8. I watched Liz Truss on a video, in a calm and considered way say that to launch nuclear weapons is 'an important job of the Prime Minister and I am ready to do that'. Worse than that, in my opinion, the audience applauded. These eight examples are from a much longer list from the last few days. What adjective can be used to describe such?

I do not want Ms. Truss as a Prime Minister. I want a Scottish First Minister elected by us with our elected government in full control of Scotland. In my opinion anything short of full Independence is absolute ………. (I need that new word here). From the above you must realise there is much work to be done among many of our fellow Scots for some of them display absolute ……. (whatever that new word turns out to be).

Kwame Nkrumah

The independence of Ghana is meaningless unless it is linked-up with the total liberation of the African Continent

Turkey
Social Media Post 2022

It takes three weeks to make a habit and two years to embed it in your brain. Scotland has had three centuries to embed the habit of being a sub-satellite and one of the last remaining colonies of the English Empire. John Curtis pops up on the screen with the latest polling data and we can easily note that still many of our fellow Scots are swamped in the habit of Unionism, what else do they know? For all their lives that is what has surrounded us. The UK gov sends out a book to our Scottish children to remind them that Queen Elizabeth is still the sovereign after seventy years. One of the big news stories of the day is that the ninety-six year old can not attend the Braemar Highland Games this year so her entry in the caber tossing tournament has been given to another family member and 'Heavens to Betsy' the next Prime Minister will be crowned at Balmoral rather than in Buckingham Palace, well that should cement the Union and get us out of a habit of a life time.

The other half of us, John Curtis, is quick to point out, are still of sound-mind and our numbers are growing. We, the enlightened, have been seeing what is coming for such along time. We have seen the 'Bullet Train' on the TV and know that if the Japanese had had a say since 1964 the distance between Edinburgh and London could have been halved nearly 60 years ago.

What is coming down the tracks towards us Scottish supporters of Independence? A new Prime Minister (this seems to be true of both candidates, who have little—if any—understanding of devolution) who is prepared to insult our First Minister and belittle our Holyrood Parliament. Who is happy to keep using our natural resources and will be coming for our water any day now. Who uses our land to dump their nuclear waste and house their evil weapons of mass destruction. Who takes a couple of hundred billion from us each year and throws back less than forty billion for us to pay our bills. (Remember in the Pandemic Johnson's lot spent £37 billion on the NHS Track and Trace phone app. More than Kate Forbes had to run the entire Scottish economy.) Then tells us we are swamped in GER's deficits.

If you want to have a glimpse of our possible future take a look at Turkey, no not the sunny beaches, it's president and economy. Their population is a third bigger that the UK, they are currently running about 80% inflation. Those who have been awake will realise that the so called 'Energy Cap' will rise by 80% at the end of the month but watch out Christmas is coming and another hike is on the horizon, despite a North Sea still full of it and wind in a hoolie as I write.

Our local authority workers have settled their pay dispute using resources which had already been allocated for other purposes. As we head down Brexit street under the yoke of yet another Tory Prime Minster that the majority of Scottish people had no hand in inflicting upon the UK take a look at Turkey. There Recep Tayyip Erdogan has manipulated the laws and conventions to remain in power. He is not the only one around the world Putin in Russia and Xi-Jinping in China have done the same. Remember in the UK system people can become Prime Minister more than once Wilson, Churchill, Baldwin, MacDonald, Glastone, Cecil et al. Do not write off Johnson just yet. The British public often has it in mind that 'we'll give it a try'. Indeed a relative of mine told me that he had voted for Brexit 'To see what it would be like'! I wonder if he knows yet.

Forget the 'Bullet Train, HS2 is not coming anywhere near Scotland. The replacement funding that used to come directly from the EU, £1.5 billion, and promised by Johnson according to Alun Cairns, former Welsh Secretary, was just a deception, the 'Shared Prosperity Fund' will not be half of that and will be controlled by Westminster. We have been saddled with 'Free-ports', green though ours maybe, but there is a strange odour about them if you ask me.

We who wish for Scottish Independence have just over a year to help people who are locked into the Unionist frame of mind to form new habits—maybe they should 'give it a try' could be a slogan?

In the world today there are 43 sovereign states with a monarch and fifteen of those share Queen Elizabeth with us! Now I do not think we should mix the Independence debate with changing to a different kind of Head of State. I think Independence maybe more easily won by keeping that status quo until later. There are 208 sovereign states Scotland should be 209. The old unionist habits could well see us soon with a similar set-up to that of Turkey where many cannot afford the basics and democracy has ceased. Or we could get into the new habits of low inflation and prosperity for all, where a 5-10% wage increase for some of our most vital workers is not at the expense of other parts of our budget. Does anyone want to get to grips with the habit of dealing with 80% inflation?

George Washington

The independence and liberty you possess are the work of joint efforts and common dangers, sufferings, and successes.

Cher Bonfis

Full Independence

Also published in 'The National' 27 August 2022 29

A PIECE on Stephen Noon in Wednesday's edition of *The Independent*, "Former Yes Scotland strategy chief makes case for compromise on independence", ruffles me up the wrong way.

I want Scotland to be independent of the rest of the UK. I want that independence to come about very soon. I want to have a Scottish passport before I die. I want Scotland to be a part of the European Union once more. I want my children to know that they are the offspring of our great nation and to be proud that they are.

Anything less, I believe, would be selling our children and grandchildren's future to a sorry mess of Tory, Sub-Tory (Labour) and Sub-sub Tory (LibDem) governance forever.

Really if we do not shout, scream and fight for our independence now – when Brexit is ruining the economic future and lowering our standard of living at lighting speed and the Tory party membership is the tiny electorate about to foist Truss or Sunak upon us as Prime Minister of the UK – then when on earth are we going to claim our right?

For heaven's sake, I am fed up to the back teeth with shimmering around the edges. If we are going to do it let's do it, I hate half-way houses. There should be no compromise –

independence only and roll on October 19 2023. I cannot wait to put my cross by Yes.

Sukarno

Independence can only be obtained and secured by a nation that has its spirit raging with determination: independence or death!

New King
Also published in 'The National' 25 September 2022 30

*A*ll things are quite silent, each mortal at rest, when me and my true love lay snug in one nest, when a bold set of ruffians broke into our cave and they forced my dear jewel to plough the salt wave. These lines I have on the album 'Living' by Judy Collins 1971. 'All Things are Quite Silent' a folk song which speaks of the 'Press-Ganging' of young men, enforced conscription for the Navy. The practice died out by 1835. Young men were ripped from their families, their beds and even their wedding ceremonies.

This may not be a conventional view of this subject: I remember hearing the 'Today' programme. Broadcaster Brian Redhead interviewed Prince Charles on the royal train. Prince Charles said that if people did not want him to do the job he was doing he would go and do something else.

My life has been rich and diverse I have had a full share of disasters and the odd triumph. I did not choose the circumstances of my birth. I would like to argue that all my disasters have been due to other people or extraneous circumstances. I would like to take full credit for any triumph and deny that anyone else had a hand in helping me achieve whatever minor success I think was mine. Of course it would be nonsense to make such claims. I had fortune to come across people who filled me with the feeling that I was a worthy human. I count it the greatest accidents of my birth that I was in no way born into the house of Windsor because whatever I have done in my life, whatever has happened to me it cannot be denied that for good or ill I was in some way or another a part of whatever happened were it good bad or ugly. I inherited no wealth, where I live, the clothes I wear and the food I eat have been obtained through my own industry. I have had times when bills could not be met and times when I have had an excess of funds. I was born and have lived my life in what are known as free countries. I have been able to have my own opinions and voice my pleasure and displeasure. I have been able to mark my cross on ballot papers and although many times the vote has not gone the way I would have wished I did get my chance to make my voice heard. In a world of so many voices I suspect I have lived a life that has been as free as it could possibly have been.

I would wish the same for every person born in any part of the world. However looking around one can see that such freedom is unavailable to billions of our fellow humans. People in Afghanistan, China, Russia, Myanmar form an obvious list of those who risk all if they speak out of turn or against those in power.

During this change in the UK where Queen Elizabeth has past and King Charles becomes the King of Scotland there are many who are against the monarchy's continuation. Many here in Scotland would prefer a republic and that cry is also heard in many outposts of the former British Empire. There are many who say that the Royal Family are over privileged but this is just to throw a bit of fat on the fire and see if one or two flames ignite. If a judge and jury imprison someone and it is later found that the crime was committed by another compensation has to be paid to the falsely convicted.

Charles, Anne, Andrew and Edward did not choose their parents but they were born into a prison which exists because many in the society support and many wallow in it and wish it to continue—The Monarchy. Every new wean born into that family is incarcerated within the system. The society removes the right of these 'royal' persons to be free, to be able to make their own decisions and live their own lives. If you think they can leave you are mistaken the story of the Duke of Windsor and Prince Harry shows they *can checkout but never leave* *Hotel California*.

In exchange the royals get big houses, cars and servants. Then people moan because there are poor people, homeless people and, and, and…..Many people love the idea of celebrity. They get caught up in the pomp and ceremony and the royals are the ultimate in celebrity.

So if you are angry about all the hype and you would prefer a Republic to a Monarchy, remember both ideas do cost money. Maybe though as I you will be thankful that your every breath is not documented, your every mistake is not recorded, your every misdemeanour not jumped upon and forever remembered. My age being not dissimilar to King Charles, I thank my lucky stars that I am not expected to do what he has done this past fortnight. I thank my stars I will never have to be monarch.

What would happen to the current royals if the doors were flung open and they were 'released' who knows? You may have read Sue Townsend's book the 'Queen and I'. I wonder what the then Prince Charles would have done with his life if he had been able to make other choices when he spoke with Brian Redhead.

Eventually the people were so fed up the wall around Berlin came tumbling down. If you are for a republic then shouting at the new king will not bring that about. The change, if it ever does come, will come because the society at large wishes for something different.

For those who support Independence for Scotland it will come about in similar fashion. I would respectfully suggest to those who want a republic, one step at a time. In the meantime thank your god for keeping you out of reach of the press-gangers and be happy you were never dragged away from the life you were planning and forced you to plough the salt wave....HMS Bronington, by the way, sank Friday 18 March 2016 in Birkenhead.

Cher Bonfis

Be careful switching on your TV because you may think the funeral is out of the way the BBC will be advertising the Coronation very soon!

Mahatma Gandhi

Personally I crave not for 'independence',
which I do not understand,
but I long for freedom from the English yoke. -

Kwasi Kwarteng has stuck his middle finger up at austerity Osborne

Also published in 'The National' 30 September 2022 31

In May 2010 The outgoing Labour Chief Secretary to the Treasury Liam Byre left a note saying there was no money left. Of course Gordon Brown, Scot, Labour Chancellor of the Exchequer sold 401 tons of gold whilst the price was at rock bottom a decade before. Another Scot, Labour Chancellor Alistair Darling was in charge of the treasury in 2008 when the banking crisis crunched and central banks started printing money for all they were worth, well what else could they have done? So in a sense Liam was probably right.

Then the Tory George Osborne became the UK Chancellor. One of his first moves was to create the OFFICE FOR BUDGET RESPONSIBILITY (OBR). The idea of this treasury funded organisation was offer independent analysis of the UK's public finances. Now any government could point at an 'external' organisation and say 'the OBR said it would be OK'.

Maybe you remember news broadcasts of baths full of water which represented the UK debt and there was trusty George, the plumber, trying to turn off the tap of more and more borrowing which kept that bath over flowing. It was all about austerity and paying down the debt. Three years later Standard and Poor's Fitch and Moody's decided that the UK finances were no longer triple 'A', diminishing the creditworthiness Bank of England Bonds. 2 years on and George decided to pay off the last of the debt from the first world war £1.9 billion. Actually that debt was not the original - Neville Chamberlain issued a bond in 1932 to cover that. There other debts in the back of the cupboard left from 1720 and 'South Sea Bubble' but that was rolled up in another bond by William Gladstone in 1853. George, such a look of cleanliness about him, but all he did was to issue new bonds ie. he borrowed more money to cover and he said 'it was a moment to for Britain to be proud' but all he did was to put the debt on another shelf in the same cupboard.

Mrs. May, so proper in her assertion that there is no 'Magic Money Tree', another fib, Alistair Darling had shown that there is always more money you just have to print it, or at least tap some keys on a computer at the Bank of England and so long as the balance sheet balances debt in one column and bonds in the other the DUP could have £1 billion for supporting the May Government.

Johnson really understood how money does grow on trees, provided you can pulp enough you can never run out. Sunak with his moral compass tried to keep a lid on it but circumstance left him with little choice but to make more. A lot of people got furlough money and diligently passed it on to the captains of industry by buying stuff and paying the rent.

Kwasi Kwarteng, pushed on by Prime Minister Truss, used his first budget to stuck a middle finger up to Osborn and austerity and 'so and so' to cautious Sunak. Kwartang and Truss THINK (really!) that the best thing is to give the rich a whole heap more money and make sure energy companies get a good whack. Whilst the rest of the world looks on and cannot believe what is happening—they cannot get rid of their pounds sterling holdings quick enough. The Bank of England, already struggling with inflation, cannot believe it either so they raise interest and as the pound drops and imports become more expensive, oil prices rise even more, fuelling inflation in every direction. Everybody but the members of His Majesty's Government knows that never in a month of Sundays will any money trickle down to the less well off from growth which is very unlikely to occur. Imports being more expensive their supply will slacken and that will add to more prices rises.

How is it not obvious to the most ardent Unionist that there is no one in the UK Government who has the slightest clue of what they are doing. Reckless with finance, foreign affaires, and worst of all the environment even when the founder of Cuadrilla, Chris Cornelius says that fracking will not be possible at any meaningful scale in the UK team Kwartang and Truss promote it anyway and for good measure they say to hell with planning regulations and consideration for wildlife. Just as a bonus the idea of Brexit to stop all those foreign people coming to England is under review because

Truss is 'THINKING' (Again!) that there are labour shortages!!!

The Union of the Crowns came in 1603. The Bank of England was established 1694. The Darien Scheme first expedition happened in 1698 and it is argued that the failure of the scheme was a factor which bought Scotland into the disaster of 1707 and the Act of Union. If only William Patterson had in 1691 decided that it was Scotland that required a central bank rather than England would we be in the situation we are now in?

Malcolm X

Revolution is based on land. Land is the basis of all independence. Land is the basis of freedom, justice, and equality....

Crazy Beaste
Social Media Post 2022

The human is a crazy beaste from the top 5% earners to pensioners like me. My best endeavours to understand why our species behaves as it does have come to nought. I read books but marvel at the illogic-logic of it all. Why does UK society provide Prime Ministers with such power? No one person has all the answers most success comes from team work. We know that there are experts in all fields yet we get stuck with a PM who says: 'I think this, therefore this what we will do'.

John Swinney often responds to inane Tory and Labour questions thus: 'The Government will carefully consider and set out our course of action having fully accessed all options.' Long may that rational continue for it is an indication that decisions are not just in the hands of one person, although one person might have to shoulder the responsibility in the end, we know things are being methodically considered and conclusions reached before actions are sanctioned. Life in Scotland should be a team effort and our governance should reflect that.

The power of Putin and other dictators is enough to turn one cold as their bidding incarcerates dissenters brutally squashed, whisked away or murdered on the streets. Putin's rise and manipulations are documented. Step by step he did whatever

Cher Bonfis

he had to so he could become the loathsome bully and war monger he is. Here in Scotland still sadly tethered to Westminster where the ruling party simply endow their leader with extraordinary power which is allowed to over ride experts and knowledge because the leader says 'I THINK'. Not just Truss I wonder if any one counts the number of times a leader says 'I think'.

During my studies of economics I learned One: economics is 'The study of the allocation of man/woman's scarce resources'. Two: all things to do with money and banking are based upon trust and confidence. Three: nobody is keen on being worse off then they were before. Four: most people want to be better off than they are.

There are economists, like Paul Zane Pilzer, who argue that economics is not about scarcity but abundance 'Unlimited Wealth' was the title of one of his books. Indeed he agues against what I learned in college, I was told that certain things have a 'fixed supply' land for example, Mark Twain said 'buy land they're not making it any more'. Yet Hong Kong Airport was built on reclaimed land at Chek Lap Kok which added 1% to Hong Kong's land surface!

In 1958 John Galbraith said that in affluent societies no sharp distinction can be made between luxuries and necessities. John Maynard Keynes thought that once people had all they wanted in material goods they would stop going to work. In

PB

practice we find that if a man buys a $200 dollar suit he then wants a $400 suit and so economies keep growing.

Economies grow anyway because there are always more people. You can 'force' rhubarb and hyacinths in the spring because there are limited variables, forcing growth in an economy is not so easy. The utter mess created by Kwartang and Truss has now got them into propaganda war trying to make out that there are people for growth and others against it, one wonders just how pathetic things can get.

Pilzer says that technology is more important than the supply physical resources in the story of growth, but when they turn off the gas in the winter everyone gets cold. So the Tories mess up scientific research via Brexit and give energy companies tax breaks for expanding oil and gas production.

There are many practical problems worldwide when a chancellor destroys trust and confidence. There they were the worlds investors trundling along trying to make the best of it and the 6th largest economy (UK is now behind India) suddenly without explanation says 'I think we should do this'! Trust and confidence which has supported the economic house of cards evaporates in an instant.

Maybe Truss has jumped on Pilzer's theories of 'Economic Alchemy' or the teachings of some other guru. However there is not much evidence that books filter through. Instead the

'WHAT I THINK' takes hold. This is what I KNOW: society handing such power to one person who can then override the knowledge and experiences of experts from around the world is ridiculous. It is very hard to understand the UK, having done itself the harm of Brexit and already enduring diminishing living standards, how Kwarteng can introduce a calamity of measures which will make us all even poorer. Then Truss expects impoverished people to have cash to increase demand to create growth as she decreases their spending power. No explanation of where the investment money will come from when investors have lost trust and growth worldwide has slowed. It is more likely that increased demand when there is diminished supply of goods, labour and services will simply fuel more inflation. Maybe in some imaginary economy this strategy might cause enough growth to pull us out of the hole that the Chancellor has dug but this is the real world and trust and confidence make it go around not money.

When Scotland regains Independence I would like to see written in our constitution limitations upon all leaders ensuring that the voices, skills and knowledge of experts must by law be part of all decisions made. They did that in the Pandemic. You may think the world is flat, you are free to think what you like, it makes no difference the experts can prove that it is an ellipsoid and that gravity keeps your feet on the ground. What we could say is that Truss certainly has got Brexit well and truly done as we ordinary folk are all now poorer.

PB

Question Time?
Social Media Post 2022

Entertainment? It is not even that! I have only caught glimpses and seen clips on FaceBook of Question Time. Once I changed channel and found Fiona Hyslop being *attacked* by a gang of union supporting audience members. It seemed there were no Independence or SNP supporters in the crowd. Bias is displayed in so many ways, I am sure you notice how the BBC and STV often provides an SNP and then follow with a Tory there is bias right there because the human brain records it all: but for expedience, without stimulation, a person can relay only 50% of what they heard on to another person and that 50% will the PEAKS and THE END of whatever story was told. The last thing we hear is often the thing that is the most powerful.

I came across QT last evening John Swinney, Anas Sarwar and Douglas Ross. So I watched. It is like a *cock-fight.* Referee Fiona Bruce constantly saying: "Time is short, not enough time, be brief." If she would just shut up there would be more time available. Presenters do this because they think it makes the show more exciting and keeps attention. In my day we only used that technique if the material was running thin, it was boring and there was still time to fill. What is the point of a programme called QUESTION TIME is there is no time for answers? It would be easy to have fewer questions. I cannot see how the QT format can provide anyone with real information or insight. Towards the end Fiona really wanted to get the 'fun' question from a wee loon but all the nasty adults and been shouting each other so there was only time to advertise that the next *dog-fight* in a bear pit near you soon.

A wee nervous manni got his big moment, (One would think that was something special 'I'm on the tele'. Wear a jacket and tie, polish the shoes, practice the lines before the camera was staring him down, the *Andy Warhol* moment!) He hesitated: "That nasty *Nicola Sturgeon* said: *She detests the Tories and all they stand for.* Is that not inciting hatred?" Perspiration, wobbling lips. There were no riots in George Square. Police Scotland was not overwhelmed by reportings of hate crimes. People are sensible enough to know, without it having to be told, that Nicola said these words meaning that she and many more of us find right wing Tory policy abhorrent. People are not dumb, they can distinguish policy and actions of a group from individual members of society, each individual having the right support whichever political organisation they desire.

Politics has to be the arena where we shout and holler, express our anger, exasperation and in exchange we restrain ourselves from resorting to physical violence and war. In the playground we said *'sticks and stones can break my bones but names can never hurt me.'* Life is a challenge it is not easy, people can be nasty the less robust must to be sheltered from storms but it is no good if everyone falls over just because there is a strong breeze.

I detest the Tory policies because generally they are based around making more money for the sake of it, hidden behind a corrupt idea: That there is a cake and the cake needs to be bigger so all can have a slice. We all know if the greedy did not take so much there would be enough already. In real life each of us makes our own cake. Some create giant wedding cakes with multiple tiers and they have lots of money. Others are happy to make a light airy Victoria sponge because they can be content, pay their bills and be happy. Even those on Universal Credit make their own cake and whatever income they get from the state goes to stimulate local economies. Each one of us is valuable, even at our end the funeral director can make his cake.

Government should not be in the business of making cakes. Their job is to make sure we all have a good kitchen so we can produce the cake we want to bake. The Government is there to protect the environment about us and make sure we have proper forces to protect our health and keep us safe from enemies.

I will annoy you now by a switch in metaphors the Government has to be the gardener making sure the weeds and pests do not make it impossible for the orchids to thrive.

If you are not angry with what has gone on over the past month and then all the months of the Johnson administration,

May, Cameron and Brexit. If you do not detest the mess you cannot have been paying attention.

A huge slice of QT last evening was taken over by a remark which plunged no one into poverty but did express the exasperation of many Scottish people. On the other hand the stuff which has destroyed the little amount trust and confidence which was left in the UK economy after the Brexit debacle, the subject to which some good answers are required and has cost all of us dear was lost. Last nights question should have been 'Should Truss and Kwarteng' still be in office, well half of that has been answered today.

Arin Paul

I believe the essence of the Independence Day is missing. We celebrate it like any other holiday, which is wrong. We must celebrate our independence everyday, not just on one day of the year.

We know it's NOT the economy, stupid – it's about passion, not finances

Also published in 'The National' 23 October 2022 32

16 October 2022 National Newspaper front cover headline: 'Well being case puts Scottish independence vote at 61 per cent', bombshell poll finds. I understand we all have to pay our bills however that head line tells us it is not all about money. If Independence is only about how quickly we start using the Scottish pound can there be anyone with an intelligence quotient of 75+ who thinks that being tied to the UK Government's financial strategy is a good idea?

In 2009 Independence supporting actor David Hayman played the part of a former Rock Star in an episode of Lewis. At the end of the episode there was a scene outdoors of a pond of brown water which contained a large macerator. Huge blades which chop through the water and break the surface like the fins of sharks. Inevitably someone falls in to the grim midden pool and has to be rescued. Watching our First Minister yesterday unveiling a paper on possible plans for Scotland's first steps into independence finance, that scene came to mind. A huge pool of news correspondents the knives of the macerator and Nicola offering a detailed analysis and questions proving that many did not listen, others interpretations of statements went wide of the mark whilst

some journalists seemed to have a remit from Tory party
headquarters.

2019 the SNP conference Edinburgh the Scottish Currency
group put forward an amendment to the growth commission
proposals. I and the majority voted that a new Scottish
Currency should be introduced as soon as is possible after
independence. That is what Nicola said yesterday. She added
that all these things have to go through many processes and
negotiations but she knows as well as anyone that the
transition time has to be as short because only when we have
our systems can we actually be Independent. Someone asked
her 5 or 10 years she said shorter than that. Now is the time to
debate our future. Papers are being published on all aspects of
Scottish life. Surely there is no one who could believe we are
doing all this work to make us worse off and if you think
living in the UK is the best living in the world, just what places
have you seen? 'Broad shoulders' of the UK give me a break.

Nicola is also playing a much more subtle political game than
anyone from the economic club could. She knows, as anyone
with any sense must gather, when we have independence we
will need many current Unionists to support independent
Scotland as these people will be living with us after
independence. She has been very careful about the
Monarchy, spoken of her feelings being Scottish and British
and she made plain that the Common Travel Area remains
because we have and will always be linked to our closest
physical neighbours. As for keeping the pound 'saftly saftly

cathchee monkey'. I would go straight to the Euro but that would frighten the horses - but did you notice that 19 member states of the EU, Montenegro, Kosovo, Saint Pierre and Miquelon, French Southern and Antarctic Lands, Saint-Barthélemy, Monaco, San Marino, Vatican City, Andorra, Saint Barthélemy, Saint Martin the British overseas territories of Akotiri and Dhekelia and others use the Euro, they all run their own economies. Why so hung up over the pound for a short while? Or indeed just accept the Euro. There have been twenty three currencies used in Scotland since David I.

Physical ties are one thing but the psyche in the way we think in Scotland has been generated from a different history from that of the people of England. This is not all about money, at least not for me, this is about us being Scottish as the French are French, the Italians are Italian. Unlike Nicola I have no truck with being British having to stick a GB, now UK, sticker on my car to drive in Europe is very displeasing to me. Ecosse, a Saltire and an EU flag that's me.

Richard Murphy weighed in to this debate and said he would vote NO on the economic plan as set out yesterday. I do agree with him about the Scottish Currency Groups proposals but there will be a transition time there was over the EU. The trick will be to be as strict as Michelle Barnier over the negotiation time-tables, which can begin as soon as we vote YES next October. If there were anything I would argue with Nicola about it would be about the GERS and the rUK being the continuing state taking all the assets and all the debt. Nicola said she felt it morally right that we as a new nation take on a proportion of the debt, well if that is the case we sure as heck better keep a good chunk of assets because they want the UN Security Council seat and frankly I think this is a place we could easily be ripped off again. The balance is they get all the assets and they take all the debt and leave us to start fresh.

It is simply daft to think that Scotland has not got the brains to sort out a Central Bank an a new name for the money. However we know that 'it is NOT the economy stupid'. Well being case puts Scottish independence vote at 61 per cent, it is not a financial thing it is a passion thing. Being in Scotland is good being in independent Scotland is better.

Scott Walker

You see, here in America there's a reason why we celebrate the 4th of July and not April 15th because in America we celebrate our independence from the government, not our dependence on it.

I will not Adjust My Expectations
Social Media Post 2022

'Millstone around our necks'. I thought to start this piece. Then I thought what does that mean in this era? You can buy them on eBay but in general 'wheat, mill, millstone, bread' is not now a common string of ideas. Then the Channel Four news finished, next a programme about the Bismark and World War II followed by The Lancaster Bomber and WWII. Even C4 cannot leave that war behind. Margaret Thatcher could not either 'don't give those Germans an inch if we do they will have us driving in kilometres before Frühstück Mittwoch.' So Brexit came about in a xenophobic catastrophe. Now look over your right shoulder see outside food banks, good working folk with tear filled eyes who's back breaking employment fails to fund the basics. Turn on the telly the economics guy explaining rampant inflation and increasing interest rates and about the young couple who just bought a house and now must find another £300 a month for the mortgage.

Echoes of Germany: 1931 Social Democrats were being challenged by the Nazi's, two years later Hitler was the Chancellor of Germany. He burnt the Reichstag and books, then launched his campaign against Jewish people whilst rearming his forces. He got cross when black athlete Jesse Owens won four gold medals at the 1936 Olympic games in Berlin, it did not fit his pseudoscientific ideas of the Aryan race.

PB

Six years later he had the whole world at war.

2022 we are in the middle the nightmare of politics called the Tory Party. Who have isolated us from our neighbours in Europe. Failed to replace all the trading agreements we had through the EU. They have crashed the economy so that, as a pal put it, 'the pound has less worth than a tattie scone'. Rising interest rates and prices. The first war on European soil for seventy years. Danger lurking, poor Ukrainians who can no longer switch on the light. I wonder if my expectations are to high. I remember clearly the three day week of Tory PM Heath, electricity on/off like a dysfunctional disco. The resonating sound of current Home Secretaries shouting for refugees to be flown to Rwanda. Politicians on huge salary reducing the pitiful amounts for those on Universal Credit and warning these layabouts need to get employment or better employment. No thought of how these fellow humans make it from day to day. 'Crack the whip that's what to do, get up you lazy', even if they do there is no guarantee there will be enough income to pay for their food and the heat. Dystopian? Lets frack for gas and suck up more oil...'Right wingers are not fooled by that climate rubbish. They do what they jolly well please. Lower taxes for the rich, lower benefits for the poor and pay with the credit card'. Investors saw through that, it wiped out the remaining trust and confidence they had after Brexit, so now there is really no money, 'silly little misguided island off the coast of Europe'. The cry goes up: 'come back Boris Johnson' and the rest of the world cannot stop laughing until tears of this calamity hit to ground, it is all just so totally pathetic.

Many countries are in good shape financially and politically. Scotland is saddled (saddled who uses horses now a days? – oh yes rich Tories who heat their stables and pass the bills off on MP's expenses). Scotland, has the 'mill stone' of Westminster 'saddled' to it. Denied basic democracy because the Westminster crowd want the oil and the water. We are without democratic mechanism to free ourselves. Dictators rule the world from China to Russia and North Korea and it could easily happen here. Democracy and human rights vanish as State employed thugs remove protesters from the streets. We feel ground down as if by a millstone and wonder should we adjust our expectations? Should we forget our dream of Independent Scotland and just be grateful we are not in China, Russia or Ukraine? After all Boris is fun, funnier than Putin anyway, he gave us money for the leccy bill and surely he is not like those other nasties (putting aside sending refugees to Rwanda). Oh and he only lies all the time. NO I WILL NOT ADJUST MY EXPECTATIONS Scotland must be free.

Many warnings of impending doom in the nineteen-thirties were ignored. There is much to compare this time with then. So here is a warning, the human race needs to unite to save our home from the catastrophic idea of growth, growth and more economic boom and bust. Or we will find ourselves, and I am not a religious person, in Revelations 'The Sea turns to blood and everything within it dies'.... 'The Sun scorches the Earth with intense heat and even burns some people with fire'.

Politicians should be saddled up with a millstone, all prospective candidates should be made to exist on Universal Credit for half a year before they can stand in elections.

Scots we have to raise our expectations and aspirations. We must embrace the idea that an Independent Scotland could lead the world away from doom and a to a better time for all, because the big picture is much more than economic growth. We need to scream this across our land.

Paul Kagame

Israel and Rwanda both play an active part in international organizations, including the U.N., but I think it's true that our unique experiences as nations have shaped a fierce independence that we will not relinquish.

Least cynical of persons
Social Media Post 2022

For those who read the things I write you will know just how 'even handed' I am and that I am the 'least cynical of persons'! You know that I am full of praise for the Tory party! (last time I made a joke like that some people thought I was serious!)

I am not going to tell you that this piece is a true assessment but I am wondering if this is a good summing up:-

The Tories caused the disaster of Brexit, they got lucky on the political front because the world was plunged into a awful Pandemic which stole the lives of millions. It covered some of the damage of Brexit and provides, even now, a shield to cover many unpleasant financial upsets. Then Europe found war on the continent for the first time in 70 years and many thousands are loosing their lives. The Russians disrupted the flow of oil and once again there was another smoke screen to hide Brexit in.

There were all the accusations and enquiries in and around 'Party Gate' and Boris Johnson's wallpaper and then by slight of hand, smoke and mirrors the Tories despatched Johnson and by some madness (or was it choreographed?) installed a person whom anyone of reasonable intelligence could see was not a person to whom the keys to the captains seat should have been given. So by this magic the UK has lost sight of Brexit and all it's horror and now all the blame for all the woes can be laid on the Truss/Kwarteng financial statement. What it did was to crush the last of the trust and confidence the financial markets had in Brexit Britain.

Many are now blinded by the light which shines off Sunak's teeth as he speaks—but do not be blinded, do not be fooled because his cabinet is full of the old guard and the Westminster shower of Tory MP's is the same as it has been since, it seems forever.

Sunak and his I, I, I, I, I, I, I, I, it is all about him 'look at me I am Prime Minister I can't believe it!' As it was all about Truss, all about Johnson, May and Cameron burning self ambition. 'Sleekit parcel of rogues' hiding behind speech making voices which all sound as if they are standing in a pulpit in an English country church.

He may prove me wrong but I think the shoes Mr Sunak will try to fill, I have said it before, far to big for him.

£200 billion for nuclear weapons at Faslane....I wonder how that Truss/Kwarteng BREXIT financial hole could be filled without smashing the poor and fixing the care system and making sure the health service has proper funding. I bet there are some cuts that could be made in the pile of awfulness. How about doing away with the whole evil lot.

PB

They will kid us all on that we have to tighten our belts make do and mend, then in two years time everything will suddenly be ok again and Tories will say look at the mess we have sorted out and vote us in for another five years. That is exactly what happened Cameron/Osborn austerity we have to stop all the borrowing. Johnson arrived and there was money for levelling up, and to buy a new Royal Yacht.

As I said above I do not know if that is a summery of fact or just a fantasy I have dreamed up for a story in my next novel.

My ambition is to help Scotland to Independence so I never have to write about English Tory mis-governance again.

Swami Vivekananda

Dependence is misery.
Independence is happiness.

I Paid
Social Media Post 2022

The UK state pension for me is £9352.72 for the year. I paid income taxes, and purchase taxes, and VAT Taxes, and Car Taxes, and Road Fund Taxes.....How much I paid in fuel duties would boggle the imagination the distances I had to cover.....and Council Taxes - Rates, I think they charged airport taxes sometimes. (I did not have to pay the alcohol or tobacco taxes because I do not use those) for 50 years, I even paid the UK National Insurance for the years I worked in other countries as well as paying my way in those places too. In the years I paid NI it was a mix of Self Employed and Schedule D, if I worked for a TV or film company each day I worked I was charged a full employed stamp on top and if I got a repeat fee on some work I paid again. During the time I had a company there was a big weekly contribution to NI but I forget exactly what it was now £14? I remember the lady who gave me my National Insurance Card and my Number saying that once I reached ...... but that was a lie because they changed the rules to make us work longer.....

OK I am happy for the wee bit extra support for the winter fuel and any other bones or crumbs that may fall from the table of whatever Government there happens to be .... so just to be fair let us say that the DWP will pay me £10000 during the year as my pension.

Liz Truss (whether she takes it or not) has the offer of I think £115000 per annum from now on so what they could give her in one year will take them 11.5 years to give to me (inflation well we hope that there will be some increases to navigate that and one assumes Truss will be rewarded similarly). It is not just her though... Cameron, May, Johnson, all the other ministers and Secretaries of State leave office with a bit of cash to get them by for a while....

As for Quentin Letts a mere child as yet at only 59 years. I wonder where he has squirrelled away his fortune for his latter years? (in October 2022 said on the television 'tax payers work all morning to pay their tax bills and only get around to earning for themselves in the afternoon then he said pensioners are on the take from the state') Perhaps he has yet to feel the creek and crack of aches and sores that often arrive with the pension. When you look up life expectancy remember to look up 'healthy life expectancy. I suppose the only way to make a person like him understand what life is really like would be if his stocks, and shares, savings, and pension plan were to be swept away in another Tory mismanagement of the economy and he was confronted with £10000 a year to survive on.

Me I keep working a bit and I do have a wee pension from abroad - I did paid my contributions there - but those payments exclude me from claiming the Pension Credit and I do not understand why because that came from money fairly and squarely earned outside the UK whilst I still kept up with

PB

contributions in the UK - I appreciate that I am not on the bottom of the ladder but it is not millionaire living .... The UK has some of the lowest pensions in the world.

So I am very much with you who may have been appalled when QUENTIN LETTS SAID THAT PENSIONERS ARE PEOPLE WHO TAKE FROM THE STATE. We pay tax on pension money that was taxed when we earned it and when they suggest pensions are BENEFITS I want to blow a gasket....

Do any of you miss a heart beat or get breathless each time they threaten the triple lock and it makes you wonder how on earth you can stretch to fill the gap if it is removed....do you ever look at the 40 and 50 year olds who are now in charge of the money and think oh my heavens? ....Oh sorry I forgot to be grateful for the bus-pass....How remiss of me sorry... and thank you SNHS for repairing me when needed.... I have written before any person wishing to be elected to a parliament should be made to live on Universal Credit for six months before they are allowed to stand...... During a working life it is not possible for everyone to take out private pensions and private health insurance, if the powers that be want that to be the norm then they have to fatten up wage packets to make it possible for ordinary folk to afford such. Why at this end of our time, when most of us have done our best, should we be subjected to threats on the value of our income?

To be called people who take from the state ....THE STATE BELONGS TO US ! IN FACT IF WE ARE NOT THE STATE OR A

PART OF IT WHAT IS THE STATE ???? The state cannot exist but for the people it serves. My blood is boiling and I want to write more but I better stop the blood pressure is well up right now.....

"Quentin Letts if your stocks and shares and bank accounts turn to mush only then will you know what it is like to be one of us"...

Pierre Bourgault

Independence must be accompanied by a social revolution

Keep on Keeping On
Social Media Post 2022

When the ALBA party began some SNP members were attracted to it. It seemed to me as if the SUPER IMPATIENT had left the IMPATIENT. To me, an IMPATIENT, things within the SNP seemed to cool down and become level-headed once more.

You may have read me write this before but the idea of a Unilateral Declaration of Independence (UDI) is a fantasy which is utterly for the birds. Physically the Anglo-Scottish border is 154 km long. There are 9910 km of coast line. We have no Army, Air force or Navy loyal to the Scottish Government and it is not conceivable that King Charles would set off Scottish Forces against English forces. Obviously the second half of that sentence is ridiculous.

The only way Scotland will become an Independent country is when a majority of the people who live in Scotland want that to happen. When that does happen, I pin my hopes on that happening soon, the other democracies who are our neighbours will recognise that and they will support it, the United Nations and the rest of the world will support it.

The SNP government are not simply there to promote independence, they are running the country for the entire five and a half million of us. Whatever way you look at it a lot of people still cling to the fantasy of the Union. The SNP try to Govern well with very limited finances and without all the

PB

leavers of power. Often things they do are then crippled by what happens in Westminster and of course the Westminster shower do not want is to go because they need us more then we need them.

If you read my stuff you know for me this is about passion. I would be happy to be poorer in my own free Scotland than to be better off in the Union—I am also convinced that all inhabitants of Scotland will see a marked rise in our living standards shortly after we become independent. If we say it is still roughly 50/50 2750000 ish of our fellow Scots are still frightened about leaving mummy Britain to fend for themselves. In polling many of them would support independence if they thought they would be better off financially and there was one wonderful poll which claimed that 61% would support Independence if it was a matter of 'Well-Being', to me the most encouraging polling yet. Lets face it the society is indoctrinated with the idea that everything is about money and how much an individual can get a hold of.

I watched some of the ALBA conference and saw Alex shouting and stamping his foot. I watched Kenny and Neale do their wee protest and Lindsay get all mad with them down in the Houses of Parliament. Then the SNP walked out of the Chamber as ALBA were to speak. All that stuff gets us no where.

The SNP show good governance, proving we can go it alone, people have to have the confidence that Scotland is well a head of the shambles of the UK administration. Our government has set up offices around the world ready, we have our own investment bank, there are plans for a stock market and our own energy company. The Trains are in public ownership we need the rails too. There are surely some folk already working on the central bank, foreign office, home office, and all the other things required in a fully independent country. Nicola Sturgeon is respected in the SNP, in Government and around the world. Opposition parties and Westminster are, in my opinion, scared to death of her because none of the current crop of politicians can hold a candle to her. The nature of our desire for independence is not the same as has been witnessed on the island of Ireland, we Scots have a different way about us.

Independence is down to you and me chatting, making pals with and taking away the fears of some of the 2750000 million Scots who have yet to feel the confidence that they will be safer, more secure and better off when Scotland becomes independent.

They will not feel that way if you get angry. They will not feel that way if you bamboozle them with facts and figures. No amount of stories about Robert the Bruce or Mary Queen of Scots will do it. The best chance for them and us is if they see the confidence and belief in your eyes when you paint a word picture of how much better we will all feel and how much better off we will all be once we are free.

Napoleon Bonaparte

Independence, like honour,
is a rocky island, without a beach.

Cher Bonfis

Blue Suede Shoes
Social Media Post 2022

Carl Perkins wrote 'Blue Suede Shoes', after seeing a dancer chide his partner for scuffing his shoes. Carl was from a family of 'sharecroppers' I could imagine him saying "hey sunshine if you knew what it took to put me in a position where I could afford to buy such shoes you would be far more respectful of my footwear."

In the 50s and early 60s the fashionable footwear for rock and roll fans were 'Winklepickers', the cause of bunion's no doubt, by the time I met a man in the autumn of 1972, who had been expelled, along with all other Asians, from Uganda by Idi Amin, the fashion for Winklepickers had died in Scotland. In Uganda the man told me they were still all the rage. The only thing this refugee had salvaged from his shoe shop was the stock, he had paid for hundreds of boxes to be shipped here only to find they were a worthless non-fashionable item. Last week King Charles hosted a reception for those Asian refugees and the television news relayed several stories of the experiences these people had and highlighted the success many of them achieved in settling and building businesses.

A couple of days later by contrast the Home Secretary flew to the Manston asylum centre by Chinook at the cost of £3500 per hour. I read about her parents, Indian heritage, moved to the UK from Mauritus and Kenya in the early 60s. Were they running from persecution, were they chasing fashionable footwear or looking for the dream of being more financially secure? I read that they liked the TV show 'Dallas' and made up Suella's name by combining the names of 2 of the characters. I never liked that programme about rich American oil tycoons who I cannot imagine would have voted Democrat. If Uma and Christie Braverman were economic migrants they did well and their daughter qualified in the law, so I ask myself why has Suella such a negative vibe regarding people who 'walk' across Africa, 'swim' the Mediterranean, 'walk' across the continent of Europe and then 'swim' the channel in search of a better life? I wonder how many of us would have the guts to do similar? What would the motivation that would have us flee our Scotland and head out into the unknown? Well we do know from our history, the 'Clearances' forced many of our forefaithers to Nova Scotia, Ontario and the Carolinas etc. Could we Scots be forced away in the future? Maybe some of us will leave if we fail in a our bid for independence next year, who of us wants to be ruled by the Tories of Westminster for the rest of our lives? Suppose there were an accident with one of those awful nuclear weapons at Faslane and Glasgow was covered in nuclear fallout. We are in the mist of a European war and a question in my mind is why has Putin ordered the evacuation of Kherson whilst advertising the idea of a 'dirty bomb' is he planning to set off a nuclear device there and produce another waste land like Chernobyl? The consequences of that could be a NATO engagement and a war that could spread the globe what with the North Koreans firing missiles and the Chinese chapping at Taiwan's door none of us can predict what mass migrations could follow from that and really no one has yet taken Climate Change seriously, although King Charles, forbidden from travelling to COP 27, held his own reception for Climate Change, as Sunak was dragged kicking to Sharm El Sheikh with his insincere smile and teleprompter of platitudes.

Suella took advantage of the Erasmus programme and then supported Brexit and so future economic migrant families to the UK no longer have that opportunity. You know if she had flown the Chinook to a beach near Calais and boarded a rubber boat and paddled across the channel like 40000 people this year I might have been able to find a bit of respect for this women but to call this an invasion and give it that edge of fascism as she did in the House of Commons last week I find despicable. Hampden Park can hold 51866. The population of Europe and here in Scotland has been shrinking because we are not making enough new weans. Loads of EU citizens returned to the continent after Brexit. Every day there are stories of labour shortages. After World War Two the Government sent out into the highways and byways to find tramps and vagabonds and offer them employment. Suddenly these people were not loafers and a drain on society they had an economic value. If the right wing would stop seeing people as a cost and would see them as a opportunity things could be so very different. Indeed I read this morning as Russian men flea Putin's draft and escape to Georgia, it has been tipped to become one of the world's fastest growing economies, now that would be 'trickle down' economics that works. 100000 Russian refugees are now in Georgia, yes there are problems, they need more houses etc, but guess what? Those Russian boys can build some. So here is a suggestion, I read in a book by Dr Denis Waitely 'The Psychology of Winning'- Chapter 1– 30 years ago, I was in Fochabers at the time. "Walk in another Indians Moccasins for a mile before passing judgment." or maybe "You can do anything but lay off of my Blue suede shoes."

Julius Nyerere

Independence cannot be real
if a nation depends upon gifts.

PB

The NHS is a marvel of healthcare that needs protecting

Also published in 'The National' 13 November 2022 33

The Hypochondriac, a play by Molière 1673 adapted by Richard Bean, I saw at Pitlochry Theatre in 1991. The story is of a perfectly healthy man who forever finds aliments to keep him in imagined sickness. 2500 years ago Hippocrates, the fellow who started the Hippocratic oath which doctors swear today, worked out that there are many people who think that they are ill when there is no sickness really. I suspect there would have been some discussion around that issue when Aneurin Bevan's team were constructing the National Health Service. Like shops there has to be a margin for those who would steal. I am sure that they factor that in their sums when setting budgets. I thought I was a hypochondriac recently. On two occasions district nurses came to my house on Sunday afternoon. I was also on the phone to the 111 service but it was not easy to see what was going on my leg, it was black and blue with bruising after a major operation and it was not until the bruises subsided that a doctor determined I had a bad infection, it took two courses of antibiotics to shift it. It is quite astonishing the advances since 1948 when the NHS started. When I was wee the measles nearly saw me aff, today the 'medicalicians' can put your whole body in a scanner and get 3D pictures of your insides. I watched 'Doctor Findly's Case Book' on the television in 1962 Tannochbrae and where I stayed back then were similar, today oh goodness they can replace bits, heart-kindney-hand-face. Personally I feel brand new and send my grateful thanks to all those who mended me and cared for me and gave me this new lease of life.

For me the Pandemic began 11 March 2020 and in the small community were I stay there were many visits from ambulances. When it was allowed I took several neighbours to many GP appointments. Amazingly since then I have had four jags to help my body fight off the Covid19 virus, I was provided with magic kits to determine if I had Covid and I have been topped up on the flu vaccine too. During the past year I have had many appointments regarding my problems and when it was realised that if I was not repaired immediately there would be no chance of repair at all they repaired me, otherwise I would now be in a wheel chair. In my small community I have heard complaints that the SNHS is not up to much. There is one person here who smokes continually and has had many visits from the ambulance services, one morning recently there were two parked outside the persons house for over an hour.

The NHS is a victim of it's own success the better it gets the more it can do, it therefore generates more and more different queues all the time. Of course if you were a government spending a lot of money on a new hospital full of the most up to date equipment it would not be much good if there were no customers! Is this a chicken and egg story or is it a

PB

egg and chicken? If fact it might be argued that a government investing in a new hospital is almost 'encouraging' people to be ill so that the facilities can been seen as a success! I know I am being a little facetious.

It is not easy to train a doctor or nurse or all the other people whose skills are required to run a health service and here we are in a Brexit induced monetary coma, short on people who have the skills and knowledge to do all this vital work. After all we all want to be fit and healthy. We all want our treatment to have started the day before yesterday and we all want to be well again after we pop one pill. For all they can do there are many cures still unavailable and we all feel sorry for our fellows who do not find what they need to restore them to health.

My bother with the opposition parties in Holyrood, and the endless drum at the beginning of STV and BBC Scottish News bulletins, which try to make it seem that the SNHS is crumbling. Sadly one can see that the Accident and Emergency services and the Ambulance services, in some parts of Scotland, are trying under the greatest pressure to do their best in circumstances which are far from ideal but the extraordinary people who work in the services are just that.

A couple of days ago the STV news reported a pilot scheme to reduce bed blocking, tonight this was again a major reason for the troubles in A&E. One person who lives near me told me I had been lucky to get surgery, I agreed but if they had not fixed me when they did I would have been beyond fixing. I am very grateful that luck came my way. Actually though I think it is not so much luck as a huge multitude of very clever people working together, the best they can under pressure, recognising where their skills were most needed at any moment, to do the best for as many people as they can. It is horrible when people do not get the treatment which they require. As usual when a part of a huge machine does not work as well as needed people shout and holler that the whole is a basket case and that it is all the Cabinet Secretary's fault.

I am very grateful for my new lease of life. I feel deeply for those who have problems still to be solved and sad for any of my fellow Scots who have not made it. When we are independent things can be better and they will be.

Wiser

Social Media Post 2022

I am certain that you have generally been wiser than me in many aspects of your life. I have spent much of mine in various messes. I have been in awe of the many brilliant people whose paths I have crossed. In younger days I had respect for those who I thought were my elders and betters. Naively I had a notion that those who formed governments, even if they were from a party I would not had chosen had knowledge and the expertise beyond that which I possessed. I thought that was why they were in the position they were in. I thought that they cared about what they were doing, that they were trying to do their best for me! Then one day I woke up. I realised that I had been sucked in by the propaganda and the media spin. Was it whilst sitting in the dark of a Ted Heath blackout? Or the scandals of the Macmillan era Christopher Vassall and John Profumo? Then Jeremy Thorpe comes to mind, him and the death of his boyfriend Norman Scott, on and on the midden heap grows and grows.

The spin and control of all the narratives through the propaganda arm of the UK government sometimes takes my breath away, I feel that there would be more real news from my compendium of Grimm's Fairy Tales, often the Grimm's stores have more morals too. It is not only in the UK, look at the spin over the stray missile into Poland. I will require a little bit more convincing to believe that a Ukrainian soldier fired a Russian made missile in an easterly direction even if he was trying to down a Russian missile. Yes I can understand NATO or the rest of us do not need this awful war to escalate, I realise lies can sometimes save us from horror. The problem is that the lines between what is a Grimm's fairy tale and what passes for BBC news bulletin are so fine it has the effect of undermining the confidence in all that supports us in society.

A few years ago there was a scandal across Europe where horse meat rather than cow meat found its way into pies and lasagne. Most people would not have noticed, some countries have butchers that specialise in horse meat, it is a delicacy. The meat was not the biggest part of the problem, it was the lie. Pies and ready made lasagne are not items I hunt for but every time I see them in the supermarket that lie is there to haunt me again. The current hiatus of a UK government was born of a midden created by Boris Johnson who was able to peddle untruths without 'a tell', I do not even think his pupils dilated. For many in society today the office of Prime Minister still holds awe and mystic, many still think that politicians are to be looked up to and that they are set to govern over us. That midden of lies though it is soft and spongy, you really do not want to fall in. The tone of the society is set by the government and it filters through in ways you might not think. For example you make an enquiry through an online form on a web site for some life insurance. A person calls you on the phone number you gave and says that they are the broker for the insurers but before they can proceed there will be security questions! They have your phone number, your name and other stuff they called you! My response is often "I have some security questions for you. What was your granny's maiden name?' There are not enough polis people in the world because the logic is the less trust that there is the more agents of social control are required. If we do not trust each other do we move to a situation where we cannot trust ourselves? Let us be honest many of us often doubt ourselves frequently.

I have no illusions of grandeur, I do not have the highest IQ in the world but I have learned that many politicians who we suffer in our dysfunctional Union are far from geniuses and sadly many are more in position to further their own life style than to better the lives of those they have been elected to represent.

Would you agree that a government should be the foundation, they should sort all the infrastructure and have the right equipment and help available when citizens have need. The government should provide the stage upon which we citizens can live our lives and get along with our business. They should be the engine and under the bonnet. Instead many of our so called leaders are pseudo celebrities, many oblivious to the needs of ordinary folk.

I know for certain that I know much more about life, economics and survival than many of the Westminster mob. By contrast I am very impressed by so many of the MPS's in our Parliament and current government, both those I have

met face to face and others whom I have seen on television. I think that what I have stated above are some of the best reasons we need Scotland to be independent and that somehow or another there needs to be a mechanism within our new constitution that protects us ordinary citizens from the likes of the Baroness of Lundin Links, who ran up an expenses tab of £15k in her first year as an un-elected peer on top of the enormous daily allowance. We need a clause that would inhibit any politician from feathering their own nest through their position as a representative of the people of Scotland......
Independence, for the people by the people.

Monty Roberts

The wonder of Independence is that it
encourages open minds
and the desire to improve.

Arrogance
Social Media Post 2022

A rrogance, is what it is, it permeates the word 'British'. Reading an history of the Third Reich you can feel it too and when Xi JinPing had former Chairman Hu Jintao removed from the Communist Party Congress, when Putin dressed down his intelligence director Sergei Naryshkin, when Trump tells his disciples that only he can make America great again and when Jeremy Hunt tells the people of the UK that global headwinds are to blame for all the economic woes, so taxes will rise to levels not experienced since1948. It is the look in his stare trying to convince me that he knows better. I wonder what the algorithm makes of his retinal scan when he enters the UK or other countries, does it say: "Wow that is the most arrogance detected since Sunak came by the other day." Another algorithm questions: "Oh no Johnson he was the most arrogant." Yet another says: "Well I had May and Truss stop by me but that Cameron with Osborn came through one after the other a few years ago and I kid you not I burnt out a possessor, I was out of action for a week!"

There he was the current Prime Minister giving a speech to the Confederation of British Industry and he sat down at a round table and pulled a silk scarf from a crystal ball and he said "I can see the future and I know that innovation will solve all our economic woes." There was a gasp from the assembled entrepreneurs, their eyes transfixed by the reflected glint from the crystal and the shining teeth of Mr. Sunak.

The PM continued: "No, no we have no need of Europe, we will not give up our right to have lower standards to our closest neighbours on the continent. No, No Mr Delore." A childhood memory of the 'supreme leader, MT' came to his mind. "We will make our own way in the world. We do not require help from anyone. We have all the people here that we need, we do not need those immigrants, unless they have first class honours degrees of course and only then when they are from really good Universities."

After the speech the English Broadcasting Corporation was there to gage the reaction of CBI members as they came around from the hypnosis, and each in turn said: "We have not got enough people. We should give limited visas until the British work force reaches the standard we require for all the complex work previous innovation has thrown up."

23 November 2022 will be an historic day and another test for the arrogance of English politics. Although it would be easier if the Judges have found that the Scottish Parliament has the competence to legislate for our referendum, if they find it has not I am sure that the numbers who will come over to the YES side of the Independence debate will be a fine and superior number. From that the call for our freedom from the arrogance parties of Westminster will become even more deafening.

The Labour leader is no better than Sunak in terms of arrogance, praised by none other than Nigel Farage on his immigration stance. Starmer could not careless about the European Union despite the majority of UK subjects polled saying leaving the EU was a mistake, but of course the EU would not allow the UK back in anytime soon, nor would they let the UK anywhere near the single market. Starmers cry to end low pay and cheap labour, I just wonder what some the folk living under the arrogance of Xi JinPing would make of that. Of course Starmer is right, workers in the UK need proper remuneration for the work that they do. As the insane arrogance of Brexit continues to cause inflation, further exacerbated by a limited number of people available to the workforce, we know that the price of labour—wages—will rise, so at least Starmer's crystal ball gives true predictions. That will fuel more inflation and before we know it there could be hyper-inflation, although the arrogant Jeremy, using his crystal ball says in two years inflation will fall, who will remember what he said two years from now?

At home in Scotland in a situation where we provide more money to the UK treasury each year than is returned in the block grant (something that never gets mentioned when the GER's deficit is banded about), it is often still difficult for those who support the Union to get a grip, they ask questions: "How would Scotland afford to be Independent?" They say it with an arrogant smirk, even though you give them whatever figures you keep in your head: "We give them £xxx billion a year they give us back £xx billion." Of course such figures are open to all sorts of interpretation and we have to be careful not to appear arrogant here but it cannot be denied that we Scots pull our weight and more. If we did not Independence would have been done long ago.

Tomorrow will not be an easy day for me, I have another week's convalescence before I am allowed to drive and my last visit to the SNHS hospital - which has NOT failed me - is tomorrow evening so I am unable to attend the rallies. I hope that you will be going because we are Scotland and we must be free from the arrogance that stalks Westminster..... For the people of Scotland by the people of Scotland.

Mahatma Gandhi

Independence means voluntary restraints and discipline, voluntary acceptance of the rule of law.

Cher Bonfis

Oil Fuelled Football
Social Media Post 2022

Qatar is small but it has oil. I have been writing about Independence for a long time. People are kind to respond with likes and comments which reveal so much and on occasion give me a chance to improve. My aim is to fit ideas on an A4 sheet, more is a bit too much to ask of the attention of you good people who engage, that length also suits The National who kindly published many of these missives. Often these pieces take a day to workout and tumble from my fingers. Sometimes they get a lot of response, one recently, I was told, went viral! I have been accused of being too strong sometimes, often when I feel I have held back, oh and not everyone agrees with some of the things I publish. Yesterday after the expected judgement on referendum legislation from the Supreme Court I wrote one line white font on a red, for danger, background, in a bold font. "I AM VERY CROSS RIGHT NOW". I do look through the responses and I try to like back, sometimes I get lost in replies to replies. I noticed one yesterday was a question mark, it is not always easy for people to pay attention I suppose! The post opened the door for a huge number of fantastic responses, so really what I want to do is say thank you for your time and for your engagement.

For me the issue of Scottish Independence has little to do with money, I remain unconvinced that money is acutely a true story. Humans invented it so they can reinvent it, they actually do – Scot-coin is an example – I believe that money is simply the tool to keep us masses in our place. The top 5% have lashings of the stuff they can come, go and do as they will. The rest of us have to come, go and do the bidding of the top 5% otherwise we have no roof, food or clothes. We are trapped in a system that is not fit for the purpose. Sumerian barley money was one of the early currencies, quite a good one as you could always eat it! Humans could not eat Cowry shells but neither could the rats, cowry shells were used as money for 4000 years, in British Uganda you could use them to pay taxes right into the 20th century. Why all the concern about what money would be used post Independence? If you want to try and grasp the absurdity of money forget about the Chancellor's yearly stand-up gig in the House of Commons if you want a real laugh take a look here https://www.ukdebtclock.co.uk/ - currently every subject (we used to be Citizens of the EU but I suspect we are now SUBJECTS of His Majesty) each of us has a debt of £35793 and the total debt increases by £5803 every second figure is £2288835XXXXX it is not possible to write the number it increases too fast. We have to maintain the illusion that money has a value—after all a house, if you have the fortune of owning one, needs to maintain it's value or rise else the bank would have nothing against which to secure your loan. All that hard earned savings, if you have the fortunate to have any, needs to retain it's value. It is however an illusion which we all have to go along with and we cannot stop because of the fear of unknown consequences.

Money is not compatible with many of the needs of humankind. The climate crisis will be solved when money is removed from the equation, that will not happen until hurricanes, floods and fires engulf seats of governance. Money will not relieve the hunger of the worlds poorest, much of the money in aid is swallowed in corruption anyway. These issues will only be resolved when everyone is understood to be valuable but as I wrote above at the moment people and things are valued in currencies.

I heard a man on the radio this morning saying that the SNP have never laid out the business case for wanting Scotland to be Independent. To me and maybe you it is obvious. I would reject the claim outright and if I had been the presenter I would have asked him: "What is the business case for remaining in the Union?"

I spoke with a woman I met this morning. I asked her what she made of the Supreme Court judgement yesterday. She hesitated and asked what I made of it. I laughed and said I asked first. Then I said it was what I had expected but that I thought it was wrong to deny democracy and that we need a fresh referendum and I want Independence. She then opened up and told me that although she had been born in England she had lived in Scotland for so long she felt Scottish and she went on to tell me how great it was here she only stopped because two pals arrived.

We are stuck in the global money machine, it suits those who have a lot of it. For me Independence supersedes money. The money and all the other things will take care of themselves because Scots are big enough, clever enough and if only we can persuade a few more Unionists of Independence we could set ourselves free we would be even more rich enough too.

I do not buy this idea that the health service is a basket case. The SNP government have upgraded and built new more than a 1000 schools. Many projects over run their budget and time frame Cross Rail and our Ferries. Our Government do the day job every day. If we only had all the levers of governance our country could provide for our citizens in the same way that many other countries provides for theirs.

"Of course Qatar has oil".

Nathan Hale

Liberty? Independence?
Are they to remain only words?
Gentlemen, let us make them fighting words!

Cher Bonfis
Deficit
Social Media Post 2022

Democratic deficit. Hardly a new concept to Scotland. There was a time when any creature, living or dead, where I stay, dressed in a red jacket with a Labour party rosette could be instantly voted into office. In the Feb 1950 General Election from the highlands to the borders the Unionist Party made the map blue but the votes from the central belt gave Labour 37 seats 46.2% of the Scottish vote, much the same as in 1945. In 1951 the Conservatives formed the UK Government 29 seats in Scotland for the Unionist Party, 35 for Labour. 1955 Anthony Eden became the Conservative Prime Minister things remained much the same in Scotland. 1959 the Scots again favoured Labour but it was Harold MacMillan, Conservative, as Prime Minister.

In 1964 Jo Grimond, Liberal, altered the situation in the Highlands but Harold Wilson, Labour, formed the UK Government with a marked increase in 43 seats for Labour from Scotland. Labour won again in 1966 with another surge from Scotland with Unionist/Conservatives having 20 seats in the House of Commons. This was a period of economic upheaval when the pound was devalued and Wilson told people, in November 1967, that the pound in their pocket was still had the same value (except you could by fewer imported products for it). Bruce Forsyth sang a pop song 'I'm Backing Britain' and some bright spark had the slogan printed on tee-shirts which were produced in Portugal!

In the General Election of1970 William Wolfe for the SNP was elected, 306802 Scots voted SNP. 1 Seat SNP, 23 seats Conservative and 44 Scottish seats for Labour.

In1974 there were two General Elections, the first in February no party won enough seats. Edward Heath failed to form a collation so there was a minority administration under Harold Wilson, who called another election in October. In the February election there had been a surge in the vote for the SNP 7 seats and a further increase to 11 seats in October. The majority of Scots voted for Labour and Wilson was the Prime Minister but only just, he had a one seat majority.

Then the tide washed in the terror of the Thatcher years, which began Feb 1975 and went on and on until Nov 1990. The SNP lost 335358 people and their votes provided Labour with 44, Conservative 22, Liberal 3, SNP 2. In 1983 The SNP voting cohort went down again Labour and Conservative hardly changed. In 1987 the Tories were squeezed and some people returned to the SNP, this is possibly one of the moments when Scots woke up to the damage Conservatives inflict as the Tories returned only 10 seats from Scotland, Labour surged to 50 but Thatcher still won over all. The Liberals flirted with the SDP as the Alliance Party and then turned into the Liberal Democrats in 1992. Paddy Ashdown and Alex Salmond were two forces pushing change in

Scotland but still the Conservatives John Major formed the UK Government but with only 11 seats from here,

Labour clear front runners in Scotland. Then the Conservatives were completely cleared from the map of Scotland in 1997.

Labour got 56 but they were in the guise of Tony Blair's reshaped New Labour and morphing into something some may have described as more Tory than the Tories. That has been much has things have been since, apart from a little flirtation with Jeremy Corbyn, the right wing Labour Party has been and will be available for voters in the next UK General Election. In the meantime here in Scotland Conservative and the Labour councils have formed collations to keep the SNP from taking control. The difference for us in Scotland in 1997 was that Conservatives were completely wiped out. The SNP got 6 Seats.

The things changed for Scotland in 1999 our own Parliament was reconvened and Labour Donald Dewer became our First Minister with 56 Labour seats in Holyrood, 35 SNP, 17 Liberal Democrat and Conservatives 18.

In 2001 Blair won a huge majority with Charles Kennedy at the head of the Liberals and John Swinney leader of the SNP trying to hold on in Westminster.

2003 Hollyrood election Labour 50, SNP 27, Lib Dems 17, Conservative 21.

2005 Tony Blair was on the wane and the hapless Gordon Brown was itching to take his place but without Blair's flare and charisma and with Browns mirco management of all the details of our lives from PAT testing for electricals to grandparents were not allowed to care for their grandchildren without being checked for suitability by the police. Oh and the little matter of Brown selling off Gold reserves, when Chancellor, at bargain basement prices because he announced the sale before it happened. Three years of him were quite enough.

2007 in Holyrood the SNP made a big break through 47 seats to Labour's 46. Alex Salmond became First Minister.

Then New Labour look alike candidate of 2010, your friend and his, call me Dave, Cameron arrived with austerity Osborn as his Chancellor. However it was not a done deal until the Lib Dems stepped into a collation with Cameron's, 'look at me I am so hip and if you close your eyes you might mistake me for being left wing, party'.

One year later and the SNP 69 seats in Holyrood to Labour's 37 and the Conservative's 15. 2011 inevitably bought us to the referendum in 2014.

2015 The Conservatives won the UK General Election and that took the UK to the Brexit referendum in 2016. It also made the SNP the third biggest party in the UK Parliament with 56 seats showing the frustration of Independence supporters. At Holyrood in 2016 the SNP 63, Conservative 31, Labour 24, Green 6, Lib Dems 5.

As hapless as Gordon Brown - Theresa May called an early General Election in 2017 she got a reduced majority and the Scottish electorate balanced the books leaving the SNP with 35 seats. Conservatives 13, Labour 7. Boris Johnson then took her job and two years later the UK voted against Jeremy Corbyn and therefore gave Johnson an obscene majority. From the Scottish people the SNP were chosen as clear winners 48 seats, Conservatives 6, Lib Dems 4 and Labour 1.

In the European Parliament elections 2019 the SNP received more votes than any other political party in Europe.

2021 Holyrood SNP 64, Conservative 31, Labour 22, Green 8, Lib Dem 4.

George Washington

But if we are to be told by a foreign Power . . what we shall do, and what we shall not do, we have Independence yet to seek, and have contended hitherto for very little.

Distractions are not working as more in Scotland turn to independence
Also published in 'The National' 10 December 2022 34

I heard Sunak say things akin to these. "We have got to get inflation down, it is damaging living standards. If we give NHS workers a pay rise that will only make inflation worse." "If you Union leaders keep taking strike action we will turn union members into criminals by bringing in new laws." Effectively turning workers into slaves. "Anyone who vilifies Britain will face being de-radicalised." So you Scottish independence people better watch out because vilifying has not been defined. Sunak failed to point out that the reason for inflation and lack of growth is because his Tories took the UK out of the EU. The UK is adrift in a life raft having cut itself off from it's main trading partner and having failed to secure trade deals which match what it had. The rest of the world no longer cares about the UK. Cabinet members endlessly repeat 'war, Covid and Russian oil' but those things are happening to everyone in the world so everyone is in that same boat, if everyone is going through the same hiatus economically it does not mean that much. A lot of economics is about relativity. All major economies produced less and gave out free money during the Pandemic, this has been a major cause of inflation, too much money not enough good and services to soak it up. The UK has doubled down on this by choking of the supply of labour through Brexit and it's immigration policies.

A few days ago the UK sanctioned wind farms on land in England in the next breath they agreed to the opening of a new coal mine. Their propaganda said it will be good for creating jobs, yet according to every news broadcast we are told there are insufficient workers to do what already must be done. They went on to say the UK would import coke if it is not dug it up. What if folk die from 'black lung'?

Much of the produce will go for export, if only trade deals allow. Australia has a new 'greener' government and they have plenty of mines, I do not know if the Cumbrian coke will fit into their economy but if the sulphur content is the deal breaker, as it could be in England, it seems to me that the product could be hard to sell anywhere. A part from which what kind of example does it set when the worlds on fire? Would they have announced this last summer time during a heat wave when houses in East London were being burnt to the ground? Of course it is ideal now when it is cold and those nostalgic memories of the fire in the grate are so easily invoked. A few weeks ago they announced a windfall tax on the obscene profits that oil companies are making, in the same breath the government told the oil companies they could have a nice tax reduction on new production!

Keir Starer's Tory B team, grapple with his inability to emulate that charismatic thing that Blair had going. Labours poll rating has shot up because people have realised they voted for the Tories Brexit and it is this mistake which is reducing their living standards. If Starmer would try to get the EU to forgive the UK and say if the UK was good, agreeing not to rock the boat any more, could we get into the single market at least, even if they would not allow the UK full membership. Starmer still thinks that the 'red wall' will return to Labour if he supports Brexit, I think that is wrong. As for the report he commissioned from Mr. 'Hasbeen' Brown. 1. If you want the House of Lords abolished from the Scottish political landscape. 2. If you want Scotland to have borrowing powers. 3. If you want Holyrood to have a binding veto over all issues. 4. If you want more powers for Scotland. 5. If you do not want Westminster to legislate in Scotland. 6. If you want Scotland to be able to join International groups and return to the EU. 7. If you do not want Holyrood powers to be disregarded. 8. If you want the Scottish Government to have powers over foreign affaires and immigration. 9. If you want the United Kingdom to work for the people of Scotland. 10. If you want greater cooperation between governments in Pandemics and pollution. 11. If you want to create jobs in medicine and video games in Glasgow and Dundee. 12. If you want a new Council. 13. If you want Scotland to have representation in foreign affaires, transport, central bank and energy. 14. If you want to have job centres all around Scotland. 15. If you want more civil servants in Scotland. 16. If you want economic, social and constitutional innovations. 16. If you want to get out of the right wing awfulness of Tory government. 17. If you want Scotland to experience the life styles provided by so many small countries to their citizens. 18. If you want Scotland to lead the world as it has done so often over the centuries. 19. If you want citizens, refugees and who live here to be treated with the respect and to live without the burdens of poverty. 20. If you want Scotland to be governed by people that are voted into office by the Scottish electorate. 21. If you want our Scottish languages to forder (advance). All of these things and much more are available when Scotland regains it's Independence.

For me Independence is about the fundamental way I feel about my identity. I would be happy to be poorer than to live under the Raj. For many people who support the Union as they realise that Union is responsible for their diminishing standard of living their mercenary proclivity and Tory inflicted inflation will turn many of their heads towards Independence. I suspect that is partly what has cause the surge in the polls towards Independence along with those who are waking up to the deficit in Scottish democracy.

Martin Luther King, Jr.

When the architects of our republic wrote the magnificent words of the Constitution and the Declaration of Independence, they were signing a promissory note to which every American was to fall heir.

There are key issues we must fix for a post-independence economy

Also published in 'The National' 10 December 2022 35

Here are some thoughts for our independent Scottish economy. Remember the father of economics was Adam Smith of Kirkcaldy. His books 'The Theory of Moral Sentiments' (1759) and 'An Inquiry into the Nature and Causes of the Wealth of Nations' (1776) still are the foundation of economic theory. I studied the manufacture of the pin, as Mr. Smith wrote and what it tells about 'division of labour'. In economics lectures the professor told us that products are often manufactured in an area that specialises in that product. He told us that wine is best from warm climates, he said grapes were not easily produced in Scotland. He did not like my suggestion that wine could be made from fruits other than grapes, he told me not to be facetious. He said generally things get made close to the source of the raw materials. I went to those lectures many years ago and Adam Smith lived many years before that. In the world of today global shipping is a big and clever business. Today we see clever minds of brilliant people coalescing in particular spots, so products may not be produced where raw materials are but clever minds get together. Two examples in Scotland would be Dundee for computer games and Prestwick for satellites. Division of labour really means one person makes one part of something whilst another person makes another bit of it and then someone else joins the parts together. See Henry Ford, Model T Ford 1908.

Financing may be seen in a similar light. There are banks, credit unions, mortgage brokers, building societies, bonds, gilts, venture capital etc. etc. The City of London was once a leader in this field of endeavour but has seen Brexit panic-ed Jeremy Hunt loosening regulations because the city has lost it's grip on the mountain of the global financial story. The situation back in 2021 was that 440 financial service firms had left London taking £900 billion pounds of assets with them. The situation is hardly likely to be any better now.

One of the disasters of the UK economy is that much of it is run through companies financed by share holders. Many high streets are now run-down, full of betting shops, Turkish barbers and kebab take-a-ways. Before opening a 'shoppie' now, as in times before the internet, one would ask many questions like... What is the right stock? Parking, buses, trains, accessibility, insurance, theft, business rates, attracting enough customers, attracting staff, product returns, rent on the shop space, will someone trip over my door mat and sue? The responsibilities are enormous the risks vast. The thing with having great small businesses on the high street is that they provide competition for the major stores, this is where competition plays a great role in the economy. It also provides customers with choices of where and what to buy. When small independent retailers make their shops attractive they lift the spirit of anyone who passes. High streets need lots of different offers and should attract people for adventures of discovering things they may never have thought of. A good high street should lift the spirit of the people who visit. In former times towns were beautified to attract people on market day. Councils should be obliged to help as many small businesses to set up and thrive on high streets because the people of the area will feel better if they do. This should not be all just about money profit but well being too. At the moment Councils need to maximise their income from business rates. A thriving high street could offer councils other ways to get income. High streets need nice cafes, bars and restaurants. The streets need to be clean and tidy, paint work renewed, as often as required, people need to feel safe and welcomed, if all of these things were to happen high streets could be more attractive than lonely shopping online. The big shopping malls of recent time are often to expensive for small family business. The shareholders who invest in the bigger companies want a maximum return on their money and that is the point the UK economy is not balanced. Shareholders suck all the money away, new buildings might be erected when businesses are new but then they rot and are not cleaned or painted. This can be seen in social housing too where damp and mould take over because share holders take the money and the chief executive gets a huge salary whilst the workers exist on minimum wages. The low interest rates on savings in recent years have exacerbated the situation because there has been little point in a savings account for the past fifteen years so people buy shares instead. Our new Scotland needs many privately owned businesses which are not only run for profit but for pride of being the best as well.

There is a bonny wee toon called Biggar which is a nice example of a good one. Another that comes to mind is Moffat.

In a perfect housing market as demand rises suppliers come to market and profitably increase the supply, currently there is much to distort the market so it fails. Many people who own houses use them as a bank. There was a television advertisement where people were so happy with their house and neighbours until they looked a website which gave them a valuation for their property, suddenly the money changed the peoples minds and another place and new neighbours would be fine. One of the fundamental truths in economics is that things only have monetary value at the moment of sale. One way for some people to get more money is to take advantage of a rise in the value of property and re-mortgage it. A spiral then begins, people want more money so the value of their property must rise so that the bank has enough security to lend more. In many countries a house is where a home is made and a family is raised in such places capital gains taxes on houses are so huge that there is little to be gained from property price increases unless you have lived in a building for 20 years or more. Such societies, it has been argued have more stability and the people who live in them are more content. There is a slogan used by charities for homeless people 'Housing First'. If we sort out the housing market we will probably organise the homelessness situation at the same time.

Hundret Jahr of 1922
Social Media Post 2022

The 1922 committee was formed in 1923 by Conservative party Members of Parliament who were elected in 1922 it began as a dining club and things got going from there. There are 18 executive members elected by the other Conservative members of parliament. We have as part of the United Kingdom suffered this organisation for a century now. During 2022 I have heard some commentators claim that the committee has done it's job, that in other systems in other countries it would not have been so easy to oust renegade Prime Ministers as it has been in the UK during 2022. Maybe that is correct but even when this group has claimed it has done it's duty, by the submission of letters of no confidence and voting to elect a new leader, the electorate for change is extremely small and the choice of change is micro. One could also interpret their role as simply maintaining the Tory party in office even when scandals bring their government down. More recently they allowed ordinary conservative party members have a vote on new leadership candidates which did broaden the electorate but that only provided a catastrophe for the Conservatives in 2022.

It is nothing but amazing to me that in one year (you know the older you get the shorter a year becomes) the Conservatives have munched through 3 Prime Ministers and all it took was tiny fraction of the 47587254 registered voters in the UK to vote. Talk about a lack of democracy, I really do not know how one can call it a democracy with an electorate of only 141725 all from the right wing to decide who replaces their first choice failure with a new PM to be over us all.

In 2022 the Conservative and Unionist party gave the UK corruption, self-destruction and now constipation. Johnson with is wallpaper and parties, Truss with her idiotic melt down economics and now Sunak, who thinks he is so jolly clever but really needs to get off the pot because there is no motion at all now. He repeats endlessly that 'he wants to deliver', it seems that Amazon have got the government advertising their delivery services and every time Sunak appears in my thoughts I see him dressed in that brown and yellow uniform and baseball cap sported by employees of the United Parcel Service.

It is the arrogance of the Tories which drives me to distraction they waft around with the air that some god gave them the right to have dominion over the rest of us now with the Supreme Court judgement they have doubled down on their mantra of we will keep the Union intact or more accurately we want Scotland's oil, water, a place for nuclear weapons and a place to dump our nuclear waste.

What distresses me more than all of that is that with all the disasters the Tories have inflicted, the shame of Brexit and the economic devastation it continues to inflict. The half truths and out right lies pumped out through their propaganda machines, even though polls show a swing towards the support for an Independent Scotland, there are still Scots who support the Tory Party and the Union. It is of course their right in a democracy to vote for whom they please but as 2022 is replaced by 2023 I find it unbelievable that anyone could support the inertia the current UK powers pass off as governance.

So we who seek an Independent Scotland must resolve for the new 2023 that we double down and take seriously our responsibilities to engage all Scots who support the Union in conversation and find out from them why they hold the views they hold, listen intently and try to help them understand that we can and will do much better for all the people of Scotland when we restore democracy and chart a new Independent course.

Cher Bonfis

The Declaration of Arbroth 06 April 1320

From the National Records of Scotland Translation by Sir James Fergusson
(A part there of)

Quem si ab inceptis desisteret, Regi Anglorum aut Anglicis nos aut Regnum nostrum volens subicere, tanquam Inimicum nostrum et sui nostrique Juris subuersorem statim expellere niteremur et alium Regem nostrum qui ad defensionem nostram sufficeret faceremus. Quia quamdiu Centum ex nobis viui remanserint, nuncquam Anglorum dominio aliquatenus volumus subiugari. Non enim propter gloriam, diuicias aut honores pugnamus set propter libertatem solummodo quam Nemo bonus nisi simul cum vita amittit.

Yet if he should give up what he has begun, seeking to make us or our kingdom subject to the King of England or the English, we should exert ourselves at once to drive him out as our enemy and a subverter of his own right and ours, and make some other man who was well able to defend us our King; for, as long as a hundred of us remain alive, never will we on any conditions be subjected to the lordship of the English. It is in truth not for glory, nor riches, nor honours that we are fighting, but for freedom alone, which no honest man gives up but with life itself.

Cher Bonfis

Other books by

Cher Bonfis

MA WEE STORIES

This is a collection of stories written for Cher's
Instagram account. The idea was to attract an
audience for Cher's writing and hopefully entice
some people to purchase some books.
For reasons best understood by the Instagram
algorithm Cher was locked out the first account
after a post about potatoes!
That was after found three
thousand followers had been found.
A second account was begun and a similar story
happened. So we present these stories in book form.

There is a scheme which received backing from
Scottish politicians including Nicola Sturgeon and
Patrick Harvie. 'Keep the head and read!'
Read for six minutes a day and improve
Your mental health. The book has been made with
That idea in mind.

Over 150 stories

Ma Wee Stories
ISBN: Paper Back 978-1-7396723-4-8
ISBN: EBook 978-1-7396723-5-5

WHO WAS KILLED?

Douglas gave up his life, and gave all he had to
Arwyn.
Then Arwyn became involved
with Raymond.
Raymond was a policeman.
He and Arwyn
made a plan to 'execute'
Douglas and steal
his house and all his funds.
Douglas found no justice
in the English legal system, and he came
face to face with real corruption.
So who was killed?

A fantastic read from beginning to end, I cannot wait to read Cher's next book. This book was exciting and kept me wanting to turn over the next page and I'm sure other people will think of that way too.   Maureen McGuire 'Waterstons'

I always love books that can tug me in and hold me there. Read this please and then tell me when you do, because I'm dying to talk to someone about this! Highly recommended! 5/5⁕ instaws_nity 'Good Reads'

I started this story believing this was a typical psychological thriller. Much to my surprise I was taken on a very different journey, which albeit tragic, demonstrated brilliantly the altruistic nature of the main character Douglas. On occasion you want to throttle him when he fails to accept what is right in front of him but you can't help but feel affection for him at the same time.   Nicola 'Books In The Bath'

Absolutely loved this book brilliantly written, totally gripping, could not put it down, what a debut. Well done Cher Bonfis Robert A 'Amazon'

PB

I have read a lot of books. Nothing I have ever read prepared me for the emotional storm of "WHO WAS KILLED?" by Cher Bonfis. Lewis 'Amazon'

It was amazing I loved this book. Loved how the author shaped the characters and made them so real over a lifetime of humanity. It is a thriller mystery of the classic order, setting the crime scene early but leaving the reader guessing and speculating to the very end. I do believe this author a fine wordsmith but more so she has a very deep ability to get to character detail and one can witness the coming apart at the seems of human relationships. Well written, thoroughly enjoyed. Highly recommended. 5/5 Richard Harris 'Good Reads'

ISBN: Paper Back 978-1-7396723-2-4
ISBN: EBook 978-1-7396723-3-1

Cher Bonfis

WHAT HAPPENED TO KRISTOPHER ON THE ROSE TREE ESTATE?

The Bermondsey Board of Guardians purchased Shirley Lodge farm in 1899 and in 1904 they opened, what would become Shirley Oaks, a village for children who had no other place to live. The village consisted houses where the children could live. A school, a laundry, workshops, a farm and a swimming pool. The Guardians kept close supervision over the running of Shirley Oaks. In 1930 the London County Council took over until the London Boroughs were formed in 1965. Shirley Oaks was closed in 1983. In this location, and in other children's homes, and other institutions, many children found refuge and safety. There were many good and kind carers but unfortunately there were also many evil people who took advantage of their situation and subjected many children to horrific abuse. This book is an attempt to shine a broader light on the good and a brighter light on the evil.

Dedicated to all who, like me, spent their childhood
within these institutions.

Review from Amazon

The subject matter is very dark but somehow Cher Bonfis manages to bring light and breath to a very difficult subject. In great detail the life of children and young people who fall into the care of the state is bought to life in an extraordinary narrative. Very well written the text has expanded my understanding of this subject which is all to often reduced by the news media to stories of abuse by carers. The contrast between the life of Kristopher and the other youngsters is as cold to hot and what happened to him was an absolute shock. Great read, great stories wrapped up in a mystery. First class and very unusual.

ISBN: Paper Back 978-1-7396723-0-0
ISBN: EBook 978-1-7396723-0-0

Cher Bonfis

Hugh MacDiarmid

The number of people who can copulate properly may be few; the number who can write well are infinitely fewer.

Cher Bonfis

Heaven only knows what Hugh would say if he could read this book!

Cher Bonfis

61001 words

ISBN: 978-1-7396723-7-9

9 781739 672379

PB

www.ingramcontent.com/pod-product-compliance
Lightning Source LLC
Chambersburg PA
CBHW060453030426
42337CB00015B/1571